Texas Sweets
from
Grandma's Kitchen
"goodies of the past"

Recipes compiled
by Donna Duncan Jomaa

Library of Congress   87-90679

ISBN: 0-9619202-0-3

Cover Design and Graphics by Vallie Milner

Calligraphy by Sandy Rodriquez

1st Printing - January, 1988
2nd Printing - June, 1989

For additional copies write or call:

Straw Hat Productions
P. O. Box 807
Livingston, Texas 77351
(409) 967-8869

Printed by

WIMMER BROTHERS

Memphis   Dallas

2

Introduction

After many years of collecting recipes and being asked for the recipe for many of the desserts I make, I decided it was time to put them all in a book. Most of the recipes are from my Grandma's, Mary Rainwater, and my two adopted Grandmas', Hattie Sharp and Alice Lemons, recipe collections. Some are from great cooks in my family who's recipes should be shared and enjoyed by all. A few are my own creations.

My own recipe collection started with my Grandma's collection of recipes. She went to Mary Hardin Baylor College in the early 1900's, majoring in Domestic Science. She had saved her notebooks from back then with recipes given in class, of course they were fragile and browning. There were also recipes on backs of envelopes and scraps of paper, some giving only the ingredients with no instructions. The recipes I chose that I knew must have been her favorites were the ones with ingredient spots on them. Many recipes were cut from magazines and newspapers and some were sent from the gas and electric companies telling how to cook using food rations more effectively. Since some of the recipes are from war time you will notice the use of sweetners other than sugar. She also had many recipe booklets from makers of appliances of the time, most of which are no longer made.

Some of Grandma's recipes didn't always call for exact ingredients but a handful of this and a tea cup of that and a walnut or egg size of butter, a 25¢ package or a 10¢ piece of something. I had to experiment with these recipes to find out just how much to use. Like her wonderful Tea Cakes recipe calls for enough flour to be like biscuit dough. She always cooked from scratch, never using mixes to make all her desserts. Even if it takes longer, the taste is certainly worth the extra time spent.

One of the fondest memories of my childhood was our visits to Grandma's house and to see what special goodies she made for each of my sisters and me. We each had our favorites and Grandma always had a treat to please us. Christmas at Grandma's was like visiting a candy store and bake shop, except at her house you could taste and enjoy not just look and imagine the taste. I hope this cookbook will give you your own personal favorites, so you too can taste and enjoy the goodies of the past.

Dedicated to the Memory of
my Grandma,
Mary Weatherred Rainwater

with

Special Thanks to
Hattie Knight Sharp,
Alice Knight Lemons
and to all the
Special Grandmas
who have been a part of my life.

CONTENTS

from Grandma's
Bread Box

APPLE BREAD

¼ cup shortening
⅔ cup sugar
2 eggs, beaten
2 cups flour
1 teaspoon baking powder
1 teaspoon soda
1 teaspoon salt
2 cups tart apples, peeled and coarsley grated
1 teaspoon grated lemon rind
⅔ cup chopped walnuts

Cream shortening and sugar until light and fluffy. Beat in eggs. Sift dry ingredients together. Add dry ingredients alternately with the apples to the egg mixture. Stir in lemon rind and nuts. Bake in greased and floured loaf pan at 350° for 50 to 60 minutes. Cool completely before slicing.

APPLE BUTTER BREAD

2 cups flour
2 teaspoons baking powder
1 teaspoon salt
1 cup sugar
1½ teaspoons cinnamon
2 eggs
1 cup margarine, melted
1 cup apple butter
½ cup chopped pecans

Combine eggs, margarine and apple butter; beat well. Stir in pecans. Add combined dry ingredients, stirring just until ingredients are moistened. Spoon batter into greased and floured 9x5x3-inch loaf pan. Bake at 350° for 1 hour and 15 minutes or until toothpick inserted in center of loaf comes out clean. Cool 10 minutes in pan. Remove from pan and cool completely on a wire rack.

APPLESAUCE BREAD

2 cups flour
¾ cup sugar
1 teaspoon baking powder
1 teaspoon soda
1 teaspoon salt
1 teaspoon cinnamon
½ teaspoon nutmeg
½ teaspoon allspice
2 teaspoons lemon peel
1 teaspoon vanilla
½ cup margarine
1 cup applesauce
2 eggs
½ cup chopped nuts

Combine all ingredients, except nuts in a large bowl. Beat at medium speed until well blended. Stir in nuts. Pour into loaf pan which has been greased on the bottom only. Bake at 350° for 55 to 60 minutes. Cool before slicing.

GRANDMA'S APRICOT NUT LOAF

1 cup dried apricots
2 cups flour
1 cup sugar
2 teaspoons baking powder
1 teaspoon salt
¼ teaspoon soda
¼ cup shortening
1 egg
½ cup orange juice
¼ cup water
½ cup chopped pecans

In a small bowl cover apricots with warm water and let stand 15 minutes. Drain; cut into pieces. In a large mixing bowl, combine flour, sugar, baking powder, salt and soda. Add shortening, egg, juice and water. Mix until well blended. Stir in apricots and nuts. Mix well. Pour into a loaf pan that has been greased on the bottom only. Bake at 375° for 45 to 55 minutes or until toothpick inserted in the center comes out clean. Remove from pan. Cool thoroughly before slicing. Best if you let it sit for at least a day before serving. For a milder flavor use dried peaches instead of apricots.

GRANDMA'S APRICOT BREAD

⅔ cup sugar
⅓ cup shortening
2 eggs
3 tablespoons sour milk
1 cup cooked apricots
2 cups flour
1 teaspoon baking powder
½ teaspoon soda
½ teaspoon salt
1 cup chopped nuts

Blend sugar and shortening, mix well until light and fluffy. Add eggs and beat well. Stir in milk and apricots. Sift dry ingredients together and add to egg mixture. Add nuts. Stir enough to get all ingredients moistened. Pour into greased loaf pan and let stand 20 minutes. Bake at 350° for 1 hour.

BANANA BREAD

1 cup sugar
1 cup brown sugar, packed
¾ cup margarine
1 cup milk
2 eggs
3 bananas, very ripe, mashed
1 tablespoon grated orange rind
2 teaspoons baking powder
1 teaspoon soda
½ teaspoon salt
3 cups flour
1 teaspoon vanilla
1 teaspoon butter flavoring
1 cup chopped nuts

Cream sugars and margarine. Add other ingredients in order given. Beat 3 minutes. Bake in 2 greased and floured loaf pans. Bake at 350° for about 1 hour or until toothpick inserted in the center comes out clean.

This is a very good bread with a good texture.

AUNT LOUISE'S BANANA BREAD

3 cups flour
1 teaspoon soda
½ teaspoon salt
2 medium bananas, sliced
   thin
½ cup butter or margarine,
   softened
1 cup sugar
2 eggs
¼ teaspoon vanilla
¼ cup cold water
½ cup dates, finely cut up
½ cup pecans, finely
   chopped

Stir together flour, soda and salt. In a small bowl beat bananas until almost smooth. In large bowl cream butter and sugar. Beat in eggs one at a time until light and fluffy. Beat in vanilla and bananas. Add dry ingredients and beat just to blend well. Add water and beat to blend. Stir in dates and pecans. Pour into greased loaf pan. Bake at 350° for 65 to 70 minutes or until done. Let cool in pan 5 minutes; then loosen and turn onto a wire rack to cool completely.

3 C'S BREAD

3 eggs, beaten
½ cup oil
1 cup sugar
½ teaspoon salt
2½ cups flour
1 teaspoon baking powder
1 teaspoon soda
1 teaspoon cinnamon
½ cup milk
2 cups shredded carrots
1 (3½ ounce) can flake
   coconut
½ cup chopped marachino
   cherries
½ cup raisins
½ cup chopped pecans

Combine beaten eggs, oil and milk in a large bowl. Sift together dry ingredients and add to egg mixture. Mix thoroughly. Stir in carrots, coconut, cherries, raisins and nuts. Pour into greased loaf pan. Bake at 350° for 45 to 50 minutes.

CARROT BREAD

½ cup vegetable oil
½ cup buttermilk
2 eggs, slightly beaten
1 cup sugar
1½ cups flour
1 teaspoon soda
1 teaspoon cinnamon
¼ teaspoon salt
1 teaspoon vanilla
1 cup grated carrots
½ cup chopped pecans

Combine oil, buttermilk, sugar and eggs in a large mixing bowl; beat 1 minute at medium speed on electric mixer. Add combined dry ingredients; beat until moistened. Stir in vanilla, carrots and pecans. Spoon into a greased and floured loaf pan. Bake at 350° for 55 to 60 minutes or until done. Cool 10 minutes in pan. Remove from pan and cool on a wire rack.

CRANBERRY NUT BREAD

2 cups flour
1 cup sugar
1½ teaspoons baking
  powder
1 teaspoon salt
½ teaspoon soda
¾ cup orange juice
1 tablespoon grated orange
  peel
2 tablespoons shortening
1 egg
1 cup fresh cranberries,
  chopped
1 cup chopped nuts

Combine flour, sugar, baking powder, salt and soda in a large bowl. Stir to mix well. Add orange juice, orange peel, shortening and egg to the dry ingredients. Mix until well blended. Stir in cranberries and nuts. Turn into a loaf pan which has been greased on the bottom only. Bake at 350° for 55 to 65 minutes, until toothpick inserted in center comes out clean.

DATE RICH BRAN BREAD

2 cups flour
¾ cup firmly packed
  brown sugar
2 teaspoons soda
½ teaspoon salt
1½ cups bran cereal
1 cup dates, chopped
½ cup chopped pecans
1½ cups buttermilk

Combine all ingredients in a large bowl except milk. Stir well to combine. Add milk and mix well. Spoon into 3 well-greased No. 2 cans. Cover tops of cans with foil. Bake at 350° for 60 to 70 minutes, until top springs back when lightly touched in center. Remove from cans immediately.

GINGERBREAD

1 box brown sugar
1½ sticks margarine
2 cups flour
1 teaspoon nutmeg
2 eggs
1 teaspoon ginger
2 teaspoons cinnamon
1 cup buttermilk
1 teaspoon soda

Mix brown sugar, margarine and flour until mixture looks like pebbles. Reserve 1 cup of this mixture. To remaining flour mixture add nutmeg, ginger, cinnamon, buttermilk mixed with soda; then add slightly beaten eggs. Pour into greased and floured 9-inch square pan. Top with reserved cup of flour mixture. Bake at 350° for 40 minutes.

GRANDMOTHER'S GINGERBREAD

½ cup sugar
½ cup butter or margarine
1 egg
1 cup cane patch syrup
¼ teaspoon salt
2½ cups flour
1 teaspoon ginger or more
  if desired
½ teaspoon cinnamon
1½ teaspoons soda
1 cup hot water

Cream butter and sugar. Add egg and syrup and mix well. Add flour, salt and spices; beat until smooth. Mix soda into the water and add. Bake in a greased and floured 9x13-inch pan at 350° until done.

GRANDMA'S DARK GINGERBREAD

2 eggs
½ cup sugar
¾ cup molasses
⅓ cup shortening
1 cup buttermilk
2 cups flour
1 teaspoon soda
1 teaspoon baking powder
½ teaspoon salt
2 teaspoons cinnamon
2 teaspoons ginger
2 tablespoons cocoa

Beat eggs, add sugar and molasses and mix well. Mix in shortening. Mix together dry ingredients, add alternately with milk to egg mixture. Pour into a 9x13-inch greased and floured pan. Bake at 350° for 30 to 40 minutes.

AUNT LOUISE'S GINGERBREAD

½ cup butter
½ cup brown sugar, packed
1 cup molasses
3 eggs
3 cups flour
1 teaspoon cream of tartar
2 tablespoons ground ginger
1 teaspoon cinnamon
1 teaspoon ground mace
1 teaspoon nutmeg
1 teaspoon soda
½ cup milk, warm (105° to 115°)
½ cup brandy
2 tablespoons grated orange rind
⅓ cup orange juice
1 cup raisins

Cream butter, gradually add sugar, mix well. Add molasses and eggs. Combine flour, cream of tartar and spices. Dissolve soda in the warm milk. Add dry ingredients to egg mixture alternately with milk. Beat well after each addition. Add remaining ingredients and mix to combine. Pour batter into greased and floured 9x13-inch pan. Bake at 350° for 35 minutes or until done.

MAPLE NUT BREAD

1 cup maple syrup
1 cup milk
½ cup sugar
¼ cup margarine
2 egg yolks
2¼ cups flour
1 teaspoon soda
½ teaspoon salt
½ to 1 cup chopped nuts

Combine maple syrup, milk, sugar and margarine in a saucepan. Heat slowly until sugar is dissolved and margarine melts. Cool. Pour into large bowl. Sift together dry ingredients and fold into syrup mixture. Stir in nuts. Pour into a large loaf pan that has been buttered and lined with waxed paper and paper buttered. Allow to stand 15 to 20 minutes before baking. Bake at 350° for about 1¼ to 1½ hours. Cool before removing from pan.

GRAHAM CRACKER BROWN BREAD

1¾ cups flour
2 cups graham cracker
  crumbs
2 teaspoons soda
1 teaspoon salt
1 teaspoon nutmeg
½ cup shortening or
  margarine
¾ cup molasses
2 eggs
1¾ cups buttermilk
1 cup raisins

Combine all ingredients, except raisins in a large bowl. Mix at low speed until moist, beat 2 minutes at medium speed. Stir in raisins. Turn batter into a loaf pan which has been greased on the bottom only. Bake at 350° for 65 to 70 minutes or until a toothpick inserted in the center comes out clean. Remove from pan. Cool before slicing.

LEMON BREAD

1½ sticks margarine
2 cups sugar
4 eggs
½ teaspoon salt
½ teaspoon soda
3 cups flour
1 cup buttermilk
2 tablespoons grated lemon
   rind
1 cup chopped nuts

Cream margarine and sugar. Blend in eggs. Mix together dry ingredients and add alternately to egg mixture with buttermilk. Add lemon rind and nuts. Pour batter into a greased 9x5-inch loaf pan that has the bottom lined with wax paper. Bake at 300° for 40 minutes or until toothpick inserted in the center comes out clean. If the top becomes too brown before loaf is done place a piece of foil over it for remainder of baking time. Remove from oven and punch holes in bread with toothpick and pour glaze over bread while it is still hot.

Glaze:
Mix juice of 2 lemons with 1 cup of powdered sugar.

MINCEMEAT BREAD

1½ cups flour
1 cup sugar
2½ teaspoons baking
   powder
½ teaspoon salt
2 eggs, beaten
3 tablespoons shortening,
   melted and cooled
1 teaspoon vanilla
1⅓ cups ready-to-use
   mincemeat
½ cup chopped nuts

Glaze:
1 cup sifted powdered sugar
1 tablespoon milk

In large bowl sift flour, sugar, baking powder and salt. In medium bowl combine eggs, shortening and vanilla. Stir in the mincemeat and nuts. Pour egg/mincemeat mixture into dry ingredients. Stir only enough to moisten flour. Spoon batter into greased loaf pan. Bake at 350° for 1 hour or until toothpick inserted in the center comes out clean. Cool 10 minutes; remove from pan. Cool completely. Pour glaze over the top.

GRANDMA'S ORANGE MARMOLADE BREAD

¾ cup sugar
2 tablespoons shortening
1 egg
¾ cup milk
¾ cup orange marmolade
3 cups flour
3 teaspoons baking powder
1 teaspoon salt
1 teaspoon soda
1 cup chopped nuts

Mix all ingredients together until moistened. Bake in a greased loaf pan at 300° for 1 hour.

GRANDMA'S ORANGE NUT BREAD

2 cups flour
1 teaspoon baking powder
1 teaspoon soda
1 teaspoon salt
½ cup sugar
1 large orange
Boiling water
Raisins
½ cup chopped walnuts
2 tablespoons shortening, melted
½ teaspoon vanilla
2 eggs, well beaten

Sift together dry ingredients. Squeeze juice from orange; measure juice and add enough boiling water to make 1 cup. Put rind and pulp of orange through a food chopper or processor and chop fine. Measure and add raisins to make 1 cup. Combine liquid, fruit, nuts and shortening; add vanilla and eggs. Add the dry ingredients and mix only enough to moisten. Do not beat. Pour into well-greased loaf pan. Bake at 350° for about 50 minutes. Cool 5 minutes in pan before removing.

FRESH PEACH BREAD
Tastes like peach cobbler in a bread!

½ cup margarine, softened
1 cup sugar
3 eggs
2¾ cups flour
1½ teaspoons baking
  powder
½ teaspoon soda
½ teaspoon salt
1½ teaspoons cinnamon
2 cups fresh peaches,
  sliced
2 tablespoons peach
  preserves
1 teaspoon vanilla

Cream margarine and sugar. Add eggs, one at a time, beating well after each. Combine dry ingredients and add to creamed mixture alternately with peaches. Stir in preserves and vanilla. Pour batter into greased and floured 9x5x3-inch loaf pan. Bake at 350° for 1 hour or until toothpick inserted in center comes out clean. Cool in pan 10 minutes before removing. Cool completely on wire rack.

PEAR BREAD

½ cup butter
1 cup sugar
2 eggs
2 cups flour
½ teaspoon salt
½ teaspoon soda
1 teaspoon baking powder
⅛ teaspoon nutmeg
¼ cup yogurt or buttermilk
1 cup coarsely chopped
  pears
1 teaspoon vanilla

Cream butter, gradually beat in sugar. Beat in eggs one at a time. Combine dry ingredients; add to egg mixture alternately with yogurt or buttermilk. Stir in pears and vanilla. Pour into greased loaf pan. Bake at 350° for 1 hour.

PINEAPPLE NUT BREAD

4 eggs
4 cups flour
⅔ cup sugar
⅔ cup shortening, melted
2 tablespoons baking
powder
2 teaspoons salt
1½ cups chopped nuts
2 cups crushed pineapple,
undrained

Beat eggs and sugar together. Stir in melted shortening. Add sifted flour, baking powder, salt and blend well. Add nuts and pineapple, stir just enough to combine. Pour batter into 2 greased loaf pans. Bake at 350° for 1 hour. Allow 1 to 2 hours of cooling at room temperature before serving or wrapping to store in freezer.

PRUNE BREAD

1½ cups dried prunes
1½ cups flour
1 teaspoon salt
1 teaspoon baking powder
1 teaspoon soda
1 cup sugar
1 cup whole wheat flour
1 egg, beaten
1 cup buttermilk
2 tablespoons melted
shortening
½ cup chopped walnuts

Cook prunes until tender and plump; drain, reserving ½ cup of the liquid. Chop prunes. Sift together white flour, salt, soda, and baking powder; stir in sugar and whole wheat flour. Blend egg and buttermilk together; add reserved prune liquid and melted shortening and stir into dry ingredients. Stir in prunes and nuts. Spoon into a greased loaf pan. Bake at 350° for 50 to 60 minutes. Cool before removing from pan.

PUMPKIN NUT BREAD

2 cups flour
2 teaspoons baking powder
1 teaspoon soda
1 teaspoon salt
1 teaspoon cinnamon
½ teaspoon nutmeg
1 cup pumpkin
1 cup brown sugar
½ cup milk
2 eggs
½ cup softened margarine
1 cup chopped pecans

Sift together flour, baking powder, soda, salt, and spices. Combine pumpkin, sugar, milk and eggs in mixing bowl. Add dry ingredients and softened margarine. Mix until well blended. Stir in nuts. Pour batter into a well greased loaf pan. Bake at 350° for 45 to 55 minutes or until toothpick inserted in center of bread comes out clean.

For 2 loaves--Use 1 can (16 ounce) of pumpkin and double remaining ingredients. Bread freezes well.

GRANDMOTHER'S PUMPKIN BREAD

3½ cups flour
2 teaspoons soda
½ teaspoon salt
1 teaspoon cinnamon
1 teaspoon nutmeg
3 cups sugar
¾ cup oil
4 eggs
⅔ cup water
1 medium can pumpkin
1½ cups nuts

Mix ingredients in order given. Bake in a greased loaf pan at 350° for 1 hour or until done.

STRAWBERRY BREAD

2 cups margarine
3 cups sugar
2 teaspoons vanilla
½ teaspoon lemon extract
8 eggs
6 cups flour
2 teaspoons salt
2 teaspoons cream of tartar
1 teaspoon soda
2 cups strawberry
  preserves
1 cup sour cream
2 cups chopped pecans

Cream margarine, sugar and extracts; add eggs, one at a time and beat well after each addition. Stir together preserves and sour cream; add to egg mixture alternately with dry ingredients. Stir in pecans. Pour batter into 4 well greased and floured loaf pans. Bake at 350° for 50 to 55 minutes.

STRAWBERRY NUT BREAD

3 cups flour
1 teaspoon soda
1 teaspoon salt
1 teaspoon cinnamon
2 cups sugar
4 eggs, beaten
1¼ cups oil
2 (10 ounce) packages
  frozen strawberries,
  thawed, reserving ½ cup
  of juice for spread
1¼ cups chopped pecans

Put dry ingredients in a large bowl. Combine eggs, oil, strawberries and pecans in a small bowl. Make a well in the center of dry ingredients and add liquid mixture, stirring just enough to moisten. Pour into 2 greased loaf pans. Bake at 350° for 1 hour. Let stand 5 minutes before removing from pans.

Serve with 8-ounces softened cream cheese mixed with ½ cup of the strawberry juice.

SWEET POTATO BREAD

3½ cups sugar
1 cup oil
4 eggs
2 cups mashed sweet
   potatoes
⅔ cup water
3½ cups flour
3 teaspoons soda
1½ teaspoons salt
1 teaspoon cinnamon
1 teaspoon nutmeg
1 cup nuts, chopped

Mix together sugar and oil. Add eggs, one at a time, potatoes and water. Sift together dry ingredients and add to batter. Stir in nuts. Bake at 350° for 1 hour in well greased loaf pans. Fill pans only half full.

ZUCCHINI BREAD

3 eggs, well beaten
2 cups sugar
1 cup vegetable oil
2 teaspoons vanilla
3 cups zucchini, unpeeled
   and grated
3 cups flour
1 teaspoon soda
½ teaspoon salt
1 teaspoon baking powder
1 teaspoon nutmeg
1½ teaspoons cinnamon
1 cup chopped nuts

Beat eggs; add sugar gradually and add oil while beating. Add vanilla and zucchini, mix well. Add dry ingredients and mix well. Stir in nuts. Pour batter into 2 greased and floured loaf pans. Bake at 350° for 1 hour.

PLAIN MUFFINS

1 egg
¾ cup milk
⅓ cup cooking oil
1¾ cups flour
¼ cup sugar
2½ teaspoons baking
  powder
¾ teaspoon salt

In a small bowl slightly beat egg with fork; beat in milk and oil. In a large bowl stir together dry ingredients, make a well in the center and add egg mixture. Stir just to moisten, it will be lumpy. Spoon into greased muffin pans about ⅔ full. Bake at 400° for 20 to 25 minutes.

To this batter you can add 1 cup of blueberries and 2 tablespoons sugar or 1 cup chopped cranberries and ¼ sugar.

BLUEBERRY MUFFINS

1 egg, lightly beaten
½ cup milk
¼ cup melted butter
1½ cups flour
½ cup sugar
2 teaspoons baking powder
½ teaspoon salt
1 cup blueberries, canned

Combine egg, milk and butter. Sift dry ingredients together then stir into egg mixture just till moist. Fold in berries and spoon batter into buttered muffin tins. Bake at 400° for 20 to 25 minutes. Makes about 8 muffins.

QUICK CRANBERRY MUFFINS

1 cup fresh cranberries,
  chopped
½ cup powdered sugar
2 cups biscuit mix
1 cup milk
2 tablespoons sugar
1 egg

Combine cranberries and sugar. Let stand to sweeten while preparing remainder of recipe. Combine biscuit mix and remaining ingredients and stir with a spoon until dry ingredients are moistened. Batter will be lumpy. Stir in the prepared cranberries. Fill greased muffin cups ⅔ full. Bake at 400° for 20 minutes. Makes 12 muffins.

SIX WEEKS BRAN MUFFINS

4 cups All-Bran cereal
2 cups hot water
1¼ cups oleo or 1 cup oil
3 cups sugar
4 eggs
1 quart buttermilk
5 cups flour
1 teaspoon salt
5 teaspoons soda
2 cups Raisin Bran
1 (8 ounce) package
   chopped dates
1 tablespoon maple
   flavoring (optional)

Mix All-Bran and water. Set aside. Cream oleo and sugar. Add eggs and buttermilk. Stir in remaining ingredients. Add All-Bran. Stir lightly to combine. Bake at 400° for 20 minutes in greased muffins tins.

The batter keeps in the refrigerator up to 6 weeks so you can have fresh muffins every day.

DOUBLE-MAPLE MUFFINS

1½ cups flour
¼ cup sugar
3 teaspoons baking powder
½ teaspoon salt
¼ cup shortening
¾ cup oatmeal
1 egg, beaten
½ cup milk
½ cup maple syrup

Sift flour, sugar, baking powder and salt. Cut in shortening until mixture resembles coarse crumbs. Stir in oatmeal. Add egg, milk and syrup; stir only until dry ingredients are moistened. Fill greased muffin cups ⅔ full. Bake at 400° for 18 to 20 minutes. Let stand a few minutes before removing from pan. Makes 12 muffins.

Glaze:
Combine 1 teaspoon soft margarine, 1 tablespoon maple syrup and ¼ cup powdered sugar; beat thoroughly. Drizzle over hot muffins.

GRANDMA'S SUNDAY MORNING MUFFINS

¼ cup butter
1 cup sugar
2 eggs
½ cup milk
2 cups flour
2 teaspoons baking powder
½ teaspoon vanilla

Mix ingredients together in order given. Stir just till moistened. Spoon into greased muffin pans about ⅔ full. Bake at 400° for 20 to 25 minutes. Makes 12 muffins.

OATMEAL APPLESAUCE MUFFINS

½ cup margarine
¾ cup brown sugar
1 egg
1 cup flour
1 teaspoon baking powder
½ teaspoon cinnamon
¼ teaspoon soda
¼ teaspoon salt
1 cup applesauce
1 cup rolled oats
½ cup raisins
½ cup chopped nuts

Cream margarine and sugar together until light and fluffy; add egg and beat at medium speed until fluffy. Stir together flour, baking powder, cinnamon, soda and salt; add alternately with the applesauce to creamed mixture. Beat at low speed to blend. Add oatmeal, raisins and nuts. Mix at low speed ½ minute to blend. Fill greased muffin tins ⅔ full. Bake at 400° for 25 to 30 minutes.

from Grandma's
Cake Plate

GRANDMA'S CUPCAKES

½ cup butter or margarine
1 cup sugar
2 eggs
½ cup milk
2 cups flour
2 teaspoons baking powder
½ teaspoon nutmeg
½ teaspoon vanilla

Cream butter with sugar. Add eggs. Mix baking powder and nutmeg in flour; add alternately with milk to egg mixture. Stir in vanilla. Spoon into muffin pans lined with paper muffin cups. Bake at 350° for about 35 minutes or until done.

BASIC WHITE CAKE

2 cups flour
1½ cups sugar
3 teaspoons baking powder
1 teaspoon salt
1 cup milk
½ cup shortening
4 egg whites
2 teaspoons vanilla

Mix all ingredients together, except egg whites and vanilla, at low speed until moistened. Beat 2 minutes at medium speed. Add egg whites and vanilla; beat 2 more minutes at medium speed. Pour batter into well greased and floured 9x13-inch pan or 2 9-inch pans. Bake at 350° for 30 to 40 minutes, depending on size of pan or until toothpick inserted in center comes out clean. Cool in pans 10 minutes before removing. Cool completely before frosting.

BASIC YELLOW CAKE

2½ cups flour
1½ cups sugar
3 teaspoons baking powder
1 teaspoon salt
1¼ cups milk
⅔ cup shortening
2 teaspoons vanilla
2 egg yolks
2 eggs

Mix all ingredients together except vanilla, egg yolks and eggs. Beat at low speed until moistened; then beat 2 minutes at medium speed. Add vanilla, egg yolks and eggs and beat 2 minutes more at medium speed. Pour batter into well greased and floured 9x13-inch pan or 2 9-inch pans. Bake at 350° for 35 or 45 minutes, depending on size of pan, or until toothpick inserted in center comes out clean. Cool in pan 10 minutes before removing. Cool completely before frosting.

EASY ONE EGG CAKE

1¼ cups flour
¾ cup sugar
2 teaspoons baking powder
½ teaspoon salt
⅔ cup milk
¼ cup shortening
1 teaspoon vanilla
1 egg

Mix together dry ingredients. Add remaining ingredients. Beat at low speed until moistened. Beat 2 minutes at medium speed. Pour batter into a well greased and floured on the bottom only of a 8 or 9-inch square pan. Bake at 350° for 35 to 40 minutes or until toothpick inserted in center comes out clean.

This makes a good cake to serve as a strawberry shortcake or with other fruit on top and whipped cream.

MRS. JONES DUMP-IT-CAKE

1 box yellow cake mix
20 ounce can crushed
   pineapple, drained
1 can cherry pie filling
1 cup pecans
2 sticks margarine, melted

Dump in order given into a 9x13-inch ungreased pan. Pour margarine over the top covering as much surface as possible. DO NOT STIR AT ANY TIME! Bake at 350° for 40 minutes or until top is completely browned. Store in refrigerator.

ITALIAN CREAM CAKE

½ cup (1 stick) margarine
   or butter
½ cup shortening
2 cups sugar
5 eggs, separated
1 teaspoon vanilla
2 cups flour
1 teaspoon soda
1 cup buttermilk
1 cup coconut
½ to 1 cup chopped pecans

Cream margarine and shortening, add sugar and beat until fluffy. Add egg yolks and vanilla. Sift together flour and soda. Add alternately with buttermilk to the sugar mixture. Stir in coconut and pecans. Fold in beaten egg whites. Pour into greased and floured cake pans. Bake at 350° for at least 25 minutes or until toothpick inserted in center of cake comes out clean. Cool slightly, remove from pans and cool completely before icing.

Icing:
8 ounces cream cheese
½ stick margarine
1 box powdered sugar
1 teaspoon vanilla

Icing:
Beat cream cheese and margarine together until smooth. Add sugar and vanilla and beat until very smooth and creamy. Spread on cake and sprinkle the top with chopped pecans or coconut.

WORLD WAR I EGGLESS - BUTTERLESS - MILKLESS CAKE

¾ cup raisins
1½ cups hot water
1 cup packed brown sugar
½ cup shortening
2¼ cups flour
2 teaspoons baking powder
¾ teaspoon allspice
½ teaspoon salt
½ teaspoon ground cloves
½ teaspoon cinnamon
¼ teaspoon soda
½ cup chopped walnuts

Combine raisins and water; let stand 15 to 20 minutes. Cream together brown sugar and shortening about 5 minutes. Mix together dry ingredients; add to creamed mixture alternately with raisin mixture. Fold in nuts. Pour into greased and floured 9-inch pan. Bake at 350° for 40 to 45 minutes. Serve with Cider Sauce spooned over each piece.

Cider Sauce:
Combine a saucepan: 2 tablespoons cornstarch, 2 tablespoons brown sugar, ¼ teaspoon cinnamon, a dash of cloves and a dash of salt. Gradually blend 1⅓ cups apple cider into mixture. Cook and stir till thickended and bubbly.

WAR CAKE - from a 1918 cook book

1 cup molasses
1 cup corn syrup
1½ cups boiling water
2 cups raisins
2 tablespoons fat
1 teaspoon salt
1 teaspoon cinnamon
½ teaspoon cloves
½ teaspoon nutmeg
3 cups flour
1 teaspoon soda
2 teaspoons baking powder

Boil first 9 ingredients. Cool, add the flour sifted with the soda and baking powder. Drop into well greased loaf tins. Bake 45 minutes in a moderately hot oven. Makes 2 loaves.

OLD-FASHIONED SKILLET UPSIDE-DOWN CAKE

½ stick margarine
1 cup brown sugar, packed
6 slices pineapple, canned
6 marachino cherries
1½ cups flour
2 teaspoons baking powder
¼ teaspoon salt
5⅓ tablespoons margarine
¾ cup sugar
2 eggs, beaten
½ cup milk
1 teaspoon almond extract

In a medium to heavy weight 10½-inch frying pan melt the ½ stick margarine slowly to avoid browning. When melted spread brown sugar evenly in pan. Place the pineapple slices in a circle around the pan with one in the center. Place a cherry in the center of each.

Cream margarine with sugar until light and fluffy. Add beaten eggs and mix throughly. Add dry ingredients alternately with milk. Add almond extract. Beat until smooth. Pour batter over fruit in frying pan. Bake at 350° about 1 hour. Remove from oven and place a cake plate over cake and grasp plate and pan and turn over. The cake must be turned as soon as it comes out of the oven.

AUNT ALICE'S FRESH APPLE CAKE

3 cups apples, peeled and diced
2 cups sugar
2 eggs
1 cup vegetable oil
3 cups flour
½ teaspoon salt
2 teaspoons soda
1 teaspoon cinnamon
½ teaspoon allspice
1 teaspoon lemon extract or ½ teaspoon maple flavoring
1 cup chopped nuts

Mix apples and sugar, let stand while preparing rest of ingredients. Beat eggs; add oil. Mix dry ingredients together and add to egg mixture. Stir in lemon extract or maple flavoring. Mix well. Stir in nuts and apples with sugar. Blend well. Pour batter into greased and floured tube pan. Bake at 325° for 1 hour or until toothpick inserted in center comes out clean.

1-2-3-4 CAKE

1 cup butter
2 cups sugar
1 teaspoon vanilla
½ teaspoon almond extract
4 eggs
3 cups flour
2 teaspoons baking powder
½ teaspoon salt
¾ cup plus 2 tablespoons
  milk

Cream butter until very soft. Gradually add sugar, creaming well, about 10 minutes. Mix in flavoring. Add eggs, one at a time, beating after each. Combine dry ingredients and add to creamed mixture alternately with milk, beating until smooth. Pour in 2 greased 9x5x3-inch loaf pans. Bake at 325° for about 60 minutes, or bake in a greased tube pan at 350° for about 60 minutes. Top with Pineapple Glaze.

Pineapple Glaze:
Heat ¼ cup pineapple juice and 2 tablespoons butter. Add to 2¼ cups powdered sugar. Mix until smooth. Pour while still warm over tops of cakes.

APPLE BUTTER SPICE CAKE

2¼ cups flour
1 cup sugar
1 teaspoon baking powder
1 teaspoon soda
½ teaspoon salt
1 teaspoon vanilla
1 cup sour cream or 1 cup
  apple spice yogurt
¾ cup apple butter
½ cup shortening or
  margarine
2 eggs

Combine dry ingredients. Mix together all other ingredients; then mix in dry ingredients. Beat 2 minutes at medium speed, scraping bowl occasionally. Pour half of batter into greased bottom only 9x13-inch pan. Sprinkle with half of topping mixture. Spoon remaining batter over topping in pan; spreading to cover. Sprinkle with remaining topping. Bake at 350° for 40 to 45 minutes, until top springs back when touched lightly in center.

Topping:
½ cup brown sugar
½ cup chopped nuts
1 teaspoon cinnamon
½ teaspoon nutmeg

Topping:
Place all in bowl and mix together well.

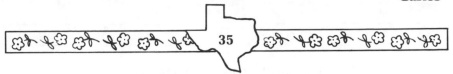
GRANDMOTHER'S APPLESAUCE CAKE

1 cup shortening
2 cups sugar
2 eggs
2 teaspoons soda dissolved in 1 teaspoon hot water
2 teaspoons cinnamon
1 teaspoon nutmeg
½ teaspoon cloves
1 teaspoon salt
3 cups flour
1 cup chopped pecans
1 cup raisins
2 cups applesauce

Cream shortening, sugar and eggs. Add soda dissolved in water. Sift dry ingredients together and add spices; mix into creamed mixture. Add pecans, raisins and applesauce. Mix well. Bake in 2 greased and floured 9-inch pans or a 9x13-pan or a tube pan. Bake at 350° until done. Frost with the following icing.

Icing for Applesauce Cake:
2 cups sugar
1 cup milk
1 stick margarine
1 cup nuts
1 cup raisins, if desired

Icing:
Cook sugar, milk and margarine in a saucepan until soft ball stage. Remove from heat and beat until creamy. Add nuts and raisins. Cool slightly before putting on cake.

FRESH BLACKBERRY CAKE

3 cups flour
2 cups sugar
1 teaspoon salt
1 teaspoon nutmeg
1 teaspoon cinnamon
½ teaspoon cloves
3 eggs, beaten
1 cup margarine, melted
1 cup buttermilk
1½ cups fresh blackberries
1 tablespoon soda
½ cup chopped nuts

Combine first 6 ingredients in a large bowl. Add eggs, margarine, buttermilk and blackberries. Beat 1 minute at medium speed on electric mixer. Stir in soda and nuts. Spoon into greased and floured bundt pan. Bake at 350° for 1 hour or until toothpick inserted comes out clean.

MINNIE'S BANANA CAKE

1½ cups sugar
½ cup oil or shortening
2 eggs
3 ripe bananas, mashed (1 cup)
½ cup buttermilk
1 teaspoon soda (dissolved in milk)
½ teaspoon salt
2 cups flour
1 teaspoon baking powder
1 teaspoon vanilla

Put dry ingredients in a large bowl. Mix together well. Form a hole in the center. Add oil or shortening, eggs, bananas, vanilla and buttermilk. Mix all together well. Pour into a 9x13-inch greased pan. Bake at 350° until done. When cool spread with the following icing.

Icing:
1 stick margarine
¼ teaspoon salt
2½ tablespoons flour
½ cup milk
½ cup brown sugar
2 cups powdered sugar
½ cup chopped pecans

Icing:
Melt margarine, stir in salt and flour. Cook 1 minute. Add milk slowly. Boil 1 minute. Stir in brown sugar and melt. While hot stir in powdered sugar and beat to spreading consistency. Stir in pecans.

BANANA SPLIT CAKE
Everyone loves this cool dessert

2 cups graham cracker crumbs
1 stick margarine, softened
3 tablespoons sugar

Mix together with fork until crumbs are moistened with margarine. Press into a 9x13-inch pan on the bottom only. Refrigerate while preparing the remaining ingredients.

2 cups powdered sugar
1 stick margarine
2 egg whites

Mix together in a small mixing bowl. Beat with electric mixer at high speed for 10 minutes. Spread over the crumbs.

1 large can crushed pineapple, well drained
4 bananas, sliced
1 large carton Cool Whip
Marachino Cherries
Chopped Pecans
Chocolate syrup

Layer pineapple over creamed mixture, put sliced bananas over pineapple, then cherries. Cover completely with Cool Whip. Sprinkle with nuts then drizzle with chocolate syrup. Refrigerate several hours then cut in squares.

GRANDMA'S BURNT SUGAR CAKE

Burnt Sugar Syrup:
½ cup sugar
⅓ cup boiling water

Burnt Sugar Syrup:
Heat sugar in a small heavy skillet, stirring as it melts. When it is dark colored and smooth, slowly add boiling water, and stir until dissolved. Cool.

Cake:
3 cups flour
3 teaspoons baking powder
¾ teaspoon salt
¾ cup butter
1 cup sugar
3 eggs, separated
1 cup milk
1 teaspoon vanilla

Cake:
Sift together flour, baking powder and salt. Cream butter and sugar, beat until light and fluffy. Add egg yolks, one at a time, beating after each. Add 3 tablespoons of the burnt sugar syrup and blend. Add flour mixture alternately with milk. Beat until smooth after each addition. Add vanilla. Beat egg whites until stiff but not dry, and stir quickly and thoroughly into the batter. Pour into 2 greased and floured 9-inch pans. Bake at 375° for 25 to 30 minutes. Let cool 5 minutes before removing from pans. When completely cool frost with Burnt Cream Frosting.

Burnt Sugar Cream Frosting:
½ cup butter
1 egg yolk
1 box powdered sugar
2 - 3 tablespoons burnt sugar syrup
2 tablespoons light cream

Burnt Sugar Cream Frosting:
Cream butter well. Add egg yolks and continue beating. Gradually add sugar and burnt sugar syrup; then add cream and beat until frosting is smooth, light and keeps its shape to spread.

CARROT CAKE

3 cups flour
1 cup sugar
1 cup brown sugar
2 teaspoons baking powder
½ teaspoon salt
1 teaspoon soda
2 teaspoons cinnamon
1½ cups vegetable oil
3 eggs, beaten
1 small can crushed
   pineapple
2 teaspoons vanilla
2 cups grated carrots
1 cup coconut
1 cup chopped pecans

Mix all dry ingredients together. Mix oil, eggs and pineapple together; then beat in dry ingredients. Add vanilla, carrots, coconut and pecans. Pour mixture into 9x13-inch greased and floured pan. Bake at 325° for about 35 minutes or until done.

MAMA'S CHOCOLATE SHEATH CAKE

1 stick margarine
4 tablespoons cocoa
1 cup water
½ cup shortening
2 cups sugar
2 cups flour
½ cup buttermilk
1 teaspoon soda
1 teaspoon salt
2 eggs
1 teaspoon vanilla

Heat margarine, cocoa, water and shortening in a saucepan until it reaches the boiling point.

Mix sugar and flour together in a mixing bowl. Pour hot mixture in. Add buttermilk with soda, salt, eggs and vanilla. Mix well. Pour batter into a 9x13-inch pan. Bake at 400° for about 20 minutes or until done. Pour Icing over the cake while it is hot.

Icing:
1 stick margarine
3 tablespoons cocoa
6 tablespoons milk
1 box powdered sugar
1 teaspoon vanilla
½ to 1 cup chopped nuts

Icing:
Heat margarine, cocoa and milk in a pan. Heat until it begins to boil. Remove from heat and add sifted powdered sugar. Blend well. Add vanilla and nuts.

TEXAS CHOCOLATE CAKE

½ cup margarine
1 cup sugar
4 eggs
1 cup flour
1 teaspoon baking powder
1 pound can Hershey
  Chocolate Syrup
1 cup pecans, chopped
1 teaspoon vanilla

Cream margarine and sugar, beat until light. Add eggs, one at a time, beating thoroughly after each. Add dry ingredients alternately with syrup, blend well. Add vanilla and nuts. Pour batter into a well greased and floured 9-inch tube pan. Bake at 350° for 45 minutes.

GRANDMA'S GERMAN CHOCOLATE CAKE

2 cups sugar
1 cup shortening
1 cup buttermilk
4 egg yolks, well beaten
2½ cups flour
1 teaspoon soda
¼ teaspoon salt
1 teaspoon vanilla
1 package German Sweet
  Chocolate dissolved in
  ½ cup boiling water
4 egg whites, beaten

Icing:
½ pint heavy cream
1 cup pecans, chopped
1 can coconut
3 egg yolks
1 cup sugar
1 stick butter

Cream sugar and shortening; add egg yolks. Add ¾ cup buttermilk alternately with flour. Put soda in remaining ¼ cup buttermilk and add to batter. Add salt. Pour in melted chocolate and mix well. Add vanilla. Fold in stiffly beaten egg whites. Pour into greased and floured 2 8 or 9-inch pans. Bake at 350° for 25 minutes. Do not over-cook. Ice with following icing between layers and on top, you can also ice around the sides.

Icing for German Chocolate Cake:
Mix ingredients together in a double boiler. Cook for 30 minutes or until the desired thickness for icing.

TRINITY RIVER MUD CAKE
There isn't any Mississippi Mud in Texas!

2 cups sugar
1 cup shortening or
 margarine
4 eggs
1½ cups flour
¼ to ½ cup cocoa
¼ teaspoon salt
3 teaspoons vanilla
2 cups chopped nuts
1 cup coconut
7 ounce jar marshmellow
 cream

Cream shortening and sugar. Add eggs. Sift together and add dry ingredients. Add vanilla, pecans and coconut. Bake in a 9x13 inch greased pan at 350° for 30 to 35 minutes. While cake is still hot spread marshmellow cream over top, then ice.

Icing:
1 stick margarine
1 box powdered sugar
⅓ cup cocoa
⅓ cup canned milk
1 teaspoon vanilla
1 cup pecans

Icing:
Heat all in a saucepan over a low heat. Cook until well mixed. Spread over marshmellow cream on cake.

CHOCOLATE CHERRY CAKE

2 cups plus 2 tablespoons
 flour
1½ cups sugar
1½ teaspoons soda
¾ teaspoon baking powder
¾ teaspoon salt
½ cup shortening
1¼ cups buttermilk or sour
 milk
2 eggs
¼ cup maraschino cherry
 juice
2 (1 ounce) squares
 chocolate, melted
⅓ cup chopped
 maraschino cherries

Combine first 5 ingredients and stir to blend. Add shortening and buttermilk. Beat 2 minutes with electric mixer. Add eggs, cherry juice and melted chocolate. Beat 2 minutes more. Stir in cherries. Pour into 2 greased and floured 9-inch pans or a 9x13-inch pan. Bake at 375° for 30 to 45 minutes, depending on size of pan. Allow to cool 15 minutes before removing from pans. Frost with Chocolate Frosting or as desired.

$100 FUDGE CAKE

½ cup butter
2 cups sugar
4 squares unsweetened
   chocolate, melted
2 eggs, beaten
2 cups flour
2 teaspoons baking powder
½ teaspoon salt
1½ cups milk
2 teaspoons vanilla
1 cup pecans, chopped

Cream butter and sugar. Add melted chocolate and eggs. Sift dry ingredients and add alternately with milk. Beat well. Add vanilla and nuts. Pour into 3 9-inch round greased and floured pans. Bake at 375° for about 45 minutes. Cool for 10 minutes in pan, then turn out on a wire rack. Frost with the following frosting.

Frosting for $100 Fudge
   Cake:
2 (1 ounce) squares
   unsweetened chocolate
½ cup butter
1 cup powdered sugar
1 egg, well beaten
1 tablespoon vanilla
1 tablespoon lemon juice
More powdered sugar
1 cup nuts, chopped

Frosting:
Melt chocolate over hot water; add butter and 1 cup powdered sugar. Beat well. Add egg, vanilla, lemon juice and enough powdered sugar to give proper spreading consistency. Add nuts. Spread on cake.

MRS. JONES' COKE CAKE

2 cups sugar
2 cups flour
1½ cups chopped
   marshmellows
1 cup margarine
3 tablespoons cocoa
1 cup Coke
½ cup buttermilk
1 teaspoon baking soda
2 eggs, beaten

Sift sugar and flour together and stir in marshmellows; set aside. Bring to a boil in a saucepan the margarine, cocoa and coke. Remove from heat and pour over dry ingredients. Stir in buttermilk, soda and eggs. Pour into greased tube pan. Bake at 350° for 45 minutes. Spread the following icing over the cooled cake.

Icing:
½ cup margarine
3 tablespoons cocoa
7 tablespoons Coke
1 box powdered sugar
1 cup pecans, chopped

Icing:
Bring margarine, cocoa and coke to a boil. When smooth remove from heat and add powdered sugar and pecans.

Cakes

AUNT ALICE'S CHOCOLATE CAKE

2 cups flour
1⅔ cups sugar
1½ teaspoons soda
1 teaspoon salt
½ teaspoon baking powder
½ cup shortening
3 squares semi-sweet
  chocolate, melted
1⅓ cups milk
3 eggs
1 teaspoon vanilla

Combine dry ingredients. Add shortening, melted chocolate and ⅔ cup milk. Blend 30 seconds, beat with mixer at medium speed for 2 minutes. Add eggs, remaining milk and vanilla. Beat 2 minutes. Spread batter in 2 well greased and floured 9-inch square pans. Bake at 350° for 30 to 35 minutes or until center springs back when touched lightly. Cool 10 to 20 minutes, then remove from pans. Frost with Coconut Pecan Frosting.

Coconut Pecan Frosting:
⅔ cup sugar
⅔ cup evaporated milk
2 egg yolks
⅓ cup margarine
½ teaspoon vanilla
1⅓ cups coconut
⅔ cup pecans, chopped

Frosting:
In a saucepan combine sugar, milk, egg yolk, margarine and vanilla. Cook and stir over medium heat until mixture comes to a boil. Remove from heat. Add coconut and pecans. Beat until thick. Cool 15 minutes. Spread only between layers and on top of cake.

MINNIE'S FIG CAKE

1½ cups sugar
3 eggs
1 cup oil
2 cups flour
1 teaspoon cinnamon
1 teaspoon nutmeg
1 cup buttermilk
1 teaspoon soda
1 cup pecans, chopped
1 cup fig preserves

Mix ingredients in order given, beating well after each addition. Pour into greased tube pan. Bake at 350° for about 1 hour and 15 minutes.

AUNT GERTRUDE'S DATE NUT CAKE

1 cup butter
4 eggs, beaten
1½ cups buttermilk
1 tablespoon grated orange
 rind
1 cup pecans, chopped
8 ounce package dates,
 chopped
2 cups sugar
4 cups flour
½ teaspoon salt
1 teaspoon soda

Cream together sugar and butter. Add eggs and beat well. Add dry ingredients alternately with buttermilk. Add orange rind, dates and pecans. Mix well. Pour into greased and floured tube pan. Bake at 325° for 1½ hours or until tested done.

When cake is done and before removing from pan, while still hot, punch many holes in cake all the way to the bottom with ice pick or skewer. Pour hot glaze over cake. Let drip in holes. If cake has not loosened from sides of pan loosen with knife so that glaze runs down the sides. Let cake stand in pan several hours or over night. Cake must be entirely cool before removing from pan.

Glaze:
1 cup orange juice
2 cups sugar
2 tablespoon grated orange
 rind

Glaze:
Dissolve sugar with juice in a saucepan. Do not allow to boil. Add rind.

AUNT JENETTE'S FRUIT CAKE

1 pound pitted dates
1 pound pecans, whole
½ pound candied cherries,
 red and green
½ pound candied green
 pineapple
1 cup sugar
4 eggs
1 cup flour
½ teaspoon salt
1 teaspoon baking powder
1 teaspoon vanilla

Cut up fruits and coat fruit and pecans with a little flour. Cream sugar and eggs until like custard. Combine dry ingredients and add to sugar mixture. Mix well. Add vanilla. Pour batter over the fruit and pecans. Stir until all is blended. Pour into 2 loaf pans lined with wax paper. Bake at 275° for 2 hours. Put a pan of water on shelf underneath the loaf pans.

TEXAS PECAN CAKE - A FRUITCAKE

3 cups sugar
3 sticks plus ½ stick
  margarine
7 eggs, separated
5 cups flour
½ cup flour to dredge fruit
  and nuts
2 ounces lemon extract
1 teaspoon soda - dissolved
  in
4 tablespoons warm wine
1 quart pecans
1 pound candied
  pineapple, cut fine
½ pound red candied
  cherries, cut fine
½ pound green candied
  cherries, cut fine

Cream sugar, margarine, egg yolks and lemon extract. Add soda and wine mixture. Add flour and mix well. Fold in fruit and nuts that have been dredged in flour. Fold in fluffy beaten egg whites. Spoon into greased loaf pan that has bottom lined with paper and greased. Bake at 250° for 4 hours or less depending on the size of pan used. Put a pan of water on the bottom shelf of the oven while the cakes are baking.

FRUIT COCKTAIL CAKE

Cake:
1½ cups sugar
2 cups flour
2 teaspoons soda
¼ teaspoon salt
2 eggs, beaten
16 ounce can fruit cocktail
1 teaspoon vanilla
1 teaspoon butter flavoring

Topping:
1 cup pecans
½ cup brown sugar

Mix all cake ingredients together. Pour batter into a greased and floured 9x13-inch pan. Combine brown sugar and pecans and sprinkle on top of cake batter. Bake at 350° for about 30 minutes. While cake is still hot, pour the following icing over the top.

Icing:
1 stick margarine
¾ cup sugar (half white
  and half brown)
½ cup milk
1 teaspoon vanilla

Icing:
Combine ingredients in a saucepan. Bring to a boil then cook for 2 minutes. Add vanilla. Pour over cake while both are still hot.

FRUIT MERINGUE DESSERT CAKE
This looks like a fancy dessert and is light.

½ cup flour
¾ teaspoon baking powder
Pinch of salt
2 eggs, separated
¾ cup sugar
¼ cup shortening
½ teaspoon vanilla
3½ tablespoons milk
Chopped Blanched
   Almonds
1 large can crushed
   pineapple or 1 pint fresh
   strawberries, sliced
1 small carton Cool Whip

Sift together flour, baking powder and salt. Beat egg yolks until thick and honey colored. Gradually beat in ¼ cup of sugar. Add shortening and vanilla. Mix well. Beat in flour mixture and milk. Beat until smooth. Spread mixture evenly between two greased layer pans. Chill about 30 minutes. Beat egg whites stiffly, fold in remaining ½ cup sugar and spread on top of each chilled cake batter. Sprinkle thickly with chopped almonds, pressing them into surface of cake batter. Bake at 300° for about 50 minutes. Cool completely. When cooled remove from pan one layer with the meringue side up on a plate. Spread with Cool Whip and place half of fruit on top. Remove other layer with meringue side up and place over the first. Spread Cool Whip on top, arrange fruit on top and sprinkle with a few almonds. Keep chilled until ready to serve.

EAST TEXAS HICKORYNUT CAKE

½ cup butter or margarine
1¼ cups sugar
2 eggs, separated
2 teaspoons vanilla
2 cups flour
3 teaspoons baking powder
¼ teaspoon salt
¾ cup milk
1 cup chopped hickory
  nuts

Cream butter with a wooden spoon. Slowly beat in sugar and beat until well blended. Add beaten egg yolks and vanilla. Add sifted ingredients alternately with milk. Fold in beaten egg whites and nuts. Pour into 2 greased 8-inch cake pans. Bake at 375° for 25 minutes. Top with the following Caramel Icing.

Carmel Icing:
2 cups sugar
1 cup milk
3 tablespoons butter
1 teaspoon vanilla
1 cup hickory nuts

Icing:
Dissolve sugar in milk and cook to desired consistency. Do not stir while cooking. Add butter and let cool without stirring. Add vanilla and nuts and stir. Spread on cake.

MAYONNAISE CAKE

1 cup mayonnaise
1½ cups sugar
2 eggs
1½ teaspoons soda
½ cup cocoa
1 cup hot water
2 cups flour
1 teaspoon vanilla

Cream mayonnaise and sugar, add eggs and mix well. In a small bowl mix soda and cocoa together, add hot water and mix well. Add to sugar mixture alternately with flour. Blend well. Stir in vanilla. Pour into greased and floured 9x13-inch pan. Bake at 350° for 30 to 35 minutes.

JAM CAKE
This is a delicious and rich cake.

1 cup butter or margarine
2 cups sugar
5 eggs
4 cups flour
¼ teaspoon salt
1½ teaspoons cloves
1½ teaspoons nutmeg
1½ teaspoons cinnamon
1½ teaspoons allspice
1 teaspoon soda
1 cup buttermilk
1 jar (18 ounce) seedless
   Blackberry Jam
1 cup chopped nuts

Cream butter and sugar; add eggs one at a time. Dissolve soda in buttermilk. Mix dry ingredients together; add to creamed mixture alternately with buttermilk. Fold in 1½ cups jam and nuts. Pour batter into 9x13-inch greased and floured pan. Bake at 350° until toothpick inserted in center of cake comes out clean. Cool completely. Cut cake in half lengthwise. Spread additional jam on bottom half then spread on half the icing over jam. Put top half on cake and ice the top.

Icing:
2 sticks margarine
2 cups sugar
1 cup milk
1 cup chopped nuts
1 cup coconut
1 teaspoon vanilla

Icing:
Cook margarine, sugar and milk in a saucepan to soft ball stage (236°) Add nuts, coconut and vanilla. Remove from heat and stir to cool slightly.

MIRACLE WHIP CHOCOLATE CAKE

2 cups flour
1 cup sugar
4 tablespoons cocoa
1½ teaspoons soda
1½ teaspoons baking
  powder
1 cup cold water
1 cup Miracle Whip
2 teaspoons vanilla

Sift together dry ingredients. Add water, Miracle Whip and vanilla. Pour into a greased and floured 9x13-inch pan. Bake at 350° for about 30 minutes. When cooled ice with the following icing.

Icing:
1 cup sugar
¼ cup cocoa
¼ cup margarine
¼ cup milk
1 teaspoon vanilla

Icing:
Mix all together in a saucepan except for vanilla. Bring to a boil and boil for one minute. Cool slightly then beat until creamy. Add vanilla. Spread on top of cake.

AUNT ALICE'S OATMEAL CAKE

1¼ cups boiling water
1 cup quick cooking
  oatmeal
½ cup butter or margarine
1 cup sugar
1 cup brown sugar
1 teaspoon vanilla
2 eggs
1½ cups flour
1 teaspoon soda
½ teaspoon salt
1 teaspoon cinnamon
½ teaspoon nutmeg

Pour water over oatmeal; cover and stand 20 minutes. Beat butter and sugars, add vanilla and eggs. Mix together dry ingredients then add to sugar mixture alternately with oatmeal and water. Mix well. Pour into greased and floured 9x13-inch pan. Bake at 350° for about 30 minutes or until toothpick inserted in center comes out clean. While hot frost with the following Broiled Frosting.

Broiled Frosting:
½ cup margarine, melted
1 cup brown sugar
¼ cup cream or canned
  milk
1 cup nuts
1 cup coconut
1 teaspoon vanilla

Frosting:
Combine all ingredients in a bowl and stir well. Spread on hot cake, then cook under broiler until bubbly.

GRANDMA'S ORANGE MARMOLADE CAKE

¾ cup butter
1 cup sugar
1 tablespoon orange rind
1 teaspoon vanilla
3 eggs
1 cup orange marmolade
1 cup chopped nuts
3 cups flour
2½ teaspoons baking
    powder
1 teaspoon salt
½ teaspoon soda
½ cup evaporated milk
½ cup orange juice

Cream butter, sugar, orange rind and vanilla. Add eggs, one at a time, beat well after each. Stir in marmolade and nuts. Sift together dry ingredients. Add to butter mixture alternately with juice and milk. Beat well. Pour into greased and floured tube pan. Bake at 350° for 1 hour. Cool cake in pan 10 minutes before removing. Glaze with powdered sugar mixed with orange juice.

AUNT ALICE'S ORANGE SLICE CAKE

1 cup butter or margarine
2 cups sugar
4 eggs
1 teaspoon soda
½ cup buttermilk
3½ cups flour
1 cup coconut
1 cup pecans, chopped
1 pound orange slice
    candy, cut up

Cream butter and sugar. Add eggs one at a time beating after each. Add buttermilk and soda. Add flour and mix well. Mix in coconut, pecans and orange slices. Pour batter into a greased and floured tube pan. Bake at 250° for 2½ to 3 hours.

Glaze:
2 cups powdered sugar
1 cup fresh orange juice

Glaze:
Combine and pour over hot cake. Let stand in pan overnight.

PEAR CAKE

4 cups fresh pears, grated
2 cups sugar
1 cup pecans, chopped
3 cups flour
1 teaspoon cinnamon
1 teaspoon nutmeg
½ teaspoon salt
½ teaspoon baking soda
1 cup vegetable oil
1 teaspoon vanilla
2 eggs, well beaten

Mix grated pears, sugar and pecans; let stand 1 hour. Mixing by hand, add dry ingredients. Then add oil, vanilla and eggs. Pour into greased and floured 11x16-inch pan or a bundt pan. Bake at 350° for about 1 hour or until done.

TEXAS PECAN CAKE

2 cups butter
2 cups sugar
6 eggs, well beaten
1 tablespoon lemon extract
4 cups flour
1½ teaspoons baking powder
2 cups raisins
4 cups pecan halves

Cream butter and sugar; add eggs and lemon extract. Add flour and baking powder, which have been sifted together and raisins and nuts stirred in. Blend well. Pour into 10-inch tube pan. Bake at 275° for 2 hours.

PERSIMMON CAKE

3 cups flour
2 cups sugar
1 teaspoon cinnamon
½ teaspoon salt
1 teaspoon soda
1 cup vegetable oil
3 eggs, beaten
1½ cups persimmon pulp
1 cup chopped walnuts
Powdered Sugar

Combine all ingredients except powdered sugar and mix well. Pour into a greased and floured 10-inch bundt pan. Bake at 325° for 1 hour or until done. Remove from pan while still warm. Dust with powdered sugar.

AUNT GERTRUDE'S TOASTED BUTTER PECAN CAKE

2 cups pecans, chopped
1¼ cups butter
3 cups flour
2 cups sugar
2 teaspoons baking powder
½ teaspoon salt
4 eggs
1 cup milk
2 teaspoons vanilla

Toast pecans in ¼ cup of butter in 350° oven for 20 to 25 minutes. Stir frequently.

Sift flour, baking powder and salt. Cream 1 cup butter, gradually add sugar, cream well. Blend in eggs, one at a time, beat after each egg. Add dry ingredients alternately with milk. Blend well. Stir in vanilla and 1⅓ cups toasted pecans. Pour into 3 9-inch pans that are grease and floured on the bottom. Bake at 350° for 25 to 30 minutes. Cool completely. Frost between layers and on top with Butter Pecan Frosting.

Butter Pecan Frosting:
Cream ¼ cup butter, add 1 box powdered sugar, 1 teaspoon vanilla and 4 to 6 tablespoons evaporated milk. Cream until spreading consistency. Stir in remaining ⅔ cup of toasted pecans.

OLD-FASHIONED PINEAPPLE CAKE

1½ cups sugar
½ cup brown sugar
2 cups flour
2 teaspoons soda
½ teaspoon salt
2 eggs
20 ounce can crushed
  pineapple with juice
½ cup nuts
1 teaspoon vanilla
1 teaspoon butter flavoring

Mix all ingredients together well. Pour into ungrease 9x13-inch pan. Bake at 350° for 25 to 35 minutes. Ice with the following icing while cake is warm.

Icing:
8 ounce package cream
  cheese, softened
½ stick margarine,
  softened
1¾ cup powdered sugar
2 teaspoons vanilla
1 cup chopped nuts
1 cup coconut

Icing:
Cream together cream cheese and margarine. Add sugar, not all one time. Add vanilla and mix until fluffy. Stir in nuts and coconut.

MRS. HOLMES' PLUM CAKE

1 cup oil
2 cups sugar
3 eggs
2 cups flour
½ teaspoon soda
Pinch of salt
2 small jars strained plums
  baby food
1 teaspoon cinnamon
½ teaspoon cloves
1 cup pecans, chopped

Mix all ingredients together well. Pour into greased tube pan. Bake at 350° for 1 hour or until done. Remove from pan and sprinkle with some powdered sugar while still hot.

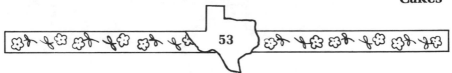

PRUNE CAKE

1 cup margarine
1 teaspoon vanilla
2 cups sugar
1 cup buttermilk
1 teaspoon soda
½ teaspoon salt
1 teaspoon cinnamon
1 teaspoon cloves
1 teaspoon allspice
3 cups flour
3 eggs
1 cup cooked pitted prunes
1 cup chopped nuts

Mix margarine, vanilla, sugar, buttermilk and soda in a large bowl. Mix salt, spice, and flour together; add to sugar mixture and beat well. Add the eggs and mix. Chop the prunes and add to batter. Add nuts and mix well. Pour into a greased 11x15-inch pan or tube pan. Bake at 350° for 30 to 60 minutes depending on size of pan. Cool for 10 minutes and remove from pan. Cool thoroughly then frost with the following frosting.

Creamy Frosting for Prune Cake:
3 ounces cream cheese, softened
6 cooked prunes, chopped
1 box powdered sugar
Milk

Mix cream cheese and prunes together. Add sugar and enough milk to give it a smooth spreading consistency. Beat until smooth then spread on cake.

GRANDMA'S 7-UP CAKE

2 sticks margarine
½ cup shortening
5 eggs
3 cups sugar
3 cups flour
¾ cup 7-Up
1 teaspoon lemon extract
1 teaspoon vanilla
1 teaspoon almond extract

Cream shortening and margarine well and add sugar a little at a time. Add eggs one at a time and beat well. Add flour alternately with 7-Up a little at a time and beat well. Add flavorings and cream well. Bake at 300° in greased and floured tube pan for about 1½ hours.

GRANDMOTHER'S NEIGHBOR'S RAISIN RUM CAKE

20 ounce can crushed
  pineapple
1½ cups sugar
½ cup butter, softened
3 eggs
1 teaspoon vanilla
1 teaspoon baking powder
½ cup green cherries,
  chopped
½ cup red cherries,
  chopped
2½ cups flour
1 teaspoon soda
1 teaspoon allspice
½ teaspoon salt
½ cup dark rum
1 cup raisins
1 cup chopped walnuts

Drain pineapple, pressing out 1¼ cups of juice, reserve ¼ cup for cake and 3 tablespoons for icing. Cream sugar and butter. Beat in eggs and vanilla. Combine flour, baking powder, soda, salt and allspice. Beat dry ingredients into butter mixture alternately with ¼ cup juice and rum. Stir in pineapple, raisins, cherries and nuts. Spoon into well grease 10-inch bundt pan. Bake at 350° for 50 to 55 minutes or until toothpick inserted comes out clean. Invert on wire rack to cool completely. Spoon Rum Glaze over cooled cake.

Rum Glaze: Beat until blended 2 or 3 tablespoons dark rum, 3 tablespoons reserved pineapple juice, 2 tablespoons softened butter and 3 cups powdered sugar. Spoon on cake and decorate top with candied cherries.

VANILLA WAFER CAKE
Grandma's recipe called for a 25¢ bag of vanilla wafers.

1 cup margarine, softened
2 cups sugar
6 eggs
½ cup milk
12 ounce box vanilla
  wafers
1 cup coconut
1 cup pecans, chopped

Crush vanilla wafers with rolling pin and set aside. Cream margarine and sugar. Beat in eggs, one at a time. Add milk and wafer crumbs. Stir in coconut and pecans. Pour into a greased and floured tube pan. Bake at 275° for 1¼ hours.

GRANDPA'S FAVORITE SPICE CAKE

½ cup butter or shortening
1½ cups white sugar or
  brown sugar, packed
1 cup sour milk
2 cups flour
1 teaspoon soda
1 teaspoon baking powder
2 teaspoons nutmeg
4 teaspoons cinnamon
1 teaspoon cloves
2 eggs
1 cup raisins
1 cup chopped nuts

Cream butter and sugar, add eggs. Mix soda into sour milk and add to sugar mixture. Sift the spices, baking powder and flour together. Add a little at a time to batter, beating smooth after each. Stir in raisins and nuts. Pour into 2 greased and floured 9-inch square pans or a 9x13-inch pan. Bake at 350° till cake is firm when touched. Frost with Carmel Icing.

Carmel Icing:
Cook 2½ cups light brown sugar with 1¼ cups cream or canned milk until it forms a soft ball when dropped in cold water. Add 1 tablespoon butter and 1 teaspoon vanilla; remove from heat and beat until it is the right consistency to spread.

STRAWBERRY JELLO CAKE

1 box white cake mix
1 (3 ounce) package
  strawberry Jello
½ cup water
½ cup vegetable oil
4 eggs
½ cup juice from 5 ounce
  carton of frozen
  sweetened
  strawberries

Combine cake mix and Jello. Add water and oil. Add eggs one at a time, beating well after each. Add juice. Bake in a greased and floured 9x13-inch pan until toothpick inserted in center of cake comes out clean. Remove from oven and cool completely.

Icing:
Sift 1 box powdered sugar and mix with 1 stick of softened margarine. Add remaining strawberries that have been mashed. Mix well. A little more powdered sugar may be needed to make it more stiff. Ice cooled cake.

BUTTERMILK POUND CAKE

2 cups sugar
1 cup shortening
4 eggs
⅛ teaspoon salt
3 cups flour
½ teaspoon baking powder
½ teaspoon soda
1 cup buttermilk
1 teaspoon vanilla
1 teaspoon lemon, orange
   or almond extract

Cream shortening, sugar, eggs and salt. Add dry ingredients alternately with buttermilk. Add flavorings. Beat together well. Spoon into greased tube pan. Bake at 300° for 1½ to 2 hours.

CORKY'S SOUR CREAM POUND CAKE

1 cup butter
3 cups sugar
6 eggs, separated
¼ teaspoon soda
3 cups flour
1 cup sour cream (½ pint)
2 teaspoons vanilla or
   lemon extract

Cream butter and sugar thoroughly. Add egg yolks one at a time. Combine flour and soda, add alternately with sour cream to butter mixture. Beat egg whites until stiff. Fold into batter. Pour into greased and floured tube pan. Bake at 300° for 1 hour and 30 minutes. Let stand for 10 minutes before removing from pan.

YOGURT POUND CAKE

1 cup (2 sticks) margarine
   or butter
2 cups sugar
4 eggs
3 cups flour
½ teaspoon soda
1 teaspoon baking powder
¼ teaspoon salt
1 cup yogurt
1 teaspoon vanilla

Cream margarine; add sugar slowly while beating. Add eggs one at a time beating after each. Sift flour three times and combine with soda, baking powder and salt. Add dry ingredients alternately with yogurt to sugar mixture. Mix in vanilla. Pour into well greased tube pan or bundt pan. Bake at 325° for 65 to 75 minutes or until it tests done.

QUICK COFFEE CAKE

¼ cup butter or margine
½ cup sugar
2 eggs, beaten well
1½ cups flour
½ teaspoon salt
2 teaspoons baking powder
1 cup milk
½ cup brown sugar
½ cup chopped pecans
1 teaspoon cinnamon
1 tablespoon margarine
1 tablespoon flour

Cream butter and sugar. Add eggs. Add dry ingredients alternately with milk. Spoon half of dough into an 8x8-inch greased pan. Combine brown sugar and remaining ingredients and sprinkle half over dough. Spoon in remaining dough and cover with remaining brown sugar-nut mixture. Bake at 350° for about 30 minutes.

QUICK CINNAMON COFFEE CAKE

4 cups biscuit mix
1 cup sugar
2 teaspoons cinnamon
½ cup chopped pecans
⅓ cup melted margarine
⅔ cup White Karo syrup

Prepare biscuit mix as shown on package. Form into 1-inch balls. Combine sugar and cinnamon; sprinkle ⅓ on bottom of greased 9 or 10-inch tube pan. Dip balls of biscuit dough in melted margarine; place, just touching, on bottom of pan. Sprinkle with ½ of sugar and ½ of nuts. Repeat a second layer. Drizzle with ⅓ cup syrup over the top. Bake at 350° for 1 hour. Invert pan and remove at once. Drizzle with remaining syrup.

LEMON COFFEE CAKE

2 tablespoons vinegar
⅞ cup canned evaporated
 milk
1 teaspoon soda
½ cup margarine, softened
1 cup sugar
2 eggs, well beaten
1 teaspoon grated lemon
 rind
1¾ cups flour
2 teaspoons baking powder
½ teaspoon salt
½ cup brown sugar, lightly
 packed
1 tablespoon cinnamon
2 tablespoons lemon juice
1 cup powdered sugar

Combine vinegar and milk in a small bowl, stir in soda. Cream margarine and sugar until fluffy; add eggs and lemon rind; beat well. Sift together dry ingredients and add alternately with milk mixture; beat well. Mix together brown sugar and cinnamon. Spread half of batter in greased and floured 10-inch tube pan; sprinkle half of cinnamon-sugar on top of batter. Pour on remaining batter and sprinkle with remaining cinnamon sugar. Bake at 350° for about 45 to 50 minutes. Cool in pan 5 minutes; remove from pan. Mix lemon juice and powdered sugar together and spoon over warm cake. Can be served warm.

CRANBERRY COFFEE CAKE

½ cup margarine
1 cup sugar
2 eggs
1 teaspoon baking powder
1 teaspoon soda
2 cups flour
½ teaspoon salt
1 cup sour cream
1 teaspoon almond extract
16 ounce can whole
 cranberry sauce
1 cup pecans, chopped

Cream margarine and sugar. Add eggs. Add dry ingredients alternately with sour cream to creamed mixture. Stir in almond extract. Pour ½ batter into greased and floured bundt pan; add ½ cranberry sauce, spread evenly over batter. Pour remaining batter over cranberry sauce then top with remaining cranberry sauce. Sprinkle with pecans. Bake at 350° for 55 minutes. Spread Glaze on cake while it is still warm.

Glaze:
1 cup powdered sugar
2 tablespoons warm water
2 teaspoons almond extract

Glaze:
Stir together well.

A GREAT AND EASY CHEESECAKE

Crust:
¾ cup butter or margarine, softened
1¼ cups flour
¼ cup sugar
1 egg yolk
Grated peel of 1 lemon

Crust:
In a small bowl beat butter at low speed. Add flour, sugar, egg yolk and grated lemon peel, beat until well mixed. Shape into ball and wrap in foil. Chill 1 hour. Press ⅓ of dough into bottom of 10-inch springform pan; bake 8 minutes at 400°. Cool. When completely cool press rest of dough around side of pan to within 1-inch of top; do not bake.

Filling:
5 (8 ounce) packages cream cheese
1¾ cups sugar
3 tablespoons flour
Grated peel of 1 lemon
2 egg yolks
5 eggs
¼ cup milk

Filling:
In a large bowl beat cream cheese just until smooth; slowly beat in sugar. With mixer at low speed beat in remaining ingredients. Beat at medium speed for 5 minutes. Pour into prepared pan; bake 12 minutes at 475° then turn oven to 300° and bake for 35 minutes longer. Turn oven off; let cheesecake remain in oven 30 minutes. Remove, cool in pan. Refrigerate until chilled. Remove from springform pan.

CHEESE CAKE

Crust:
1 stick butter
1 box Zwieback (Use one half box for each cake crust.)
2 tablespoons sugar
1 teaspoon cinnamon

Crust:
Roll zwieback into crumbs; melt butter and add to crumb base; mix in sugar and cinnamon. (Hint: This is a large cake, and the center is hard to get completely done without drying out the edges. I use an angel food cake pan that breaks apart in order to heat the center evenly. It also makes prettier slices.)

Cake:
5 eggs
4 (8 ounce) packages cream cheese
1¼ cups sugar
½ teaspoon pineapple extract
1 teaspoon vanilla

Cake:
Beat the eggs for five minutes at high speed in a mixing bowl. Break the cream cheese into small pieces and add to beaten eggs; beat at least ten minutes. Gradually add sugar, beating until blended. Add pineapple extract and vanilla and beat ten minutes longer. Pour over crust and bake at 325° for 45 minutes or until firm. Cool 30 minutes.

Topping:
1 pint sour cream
3 tablespoons sugar
½ teaspoon vanilla
½ teaspoon pineapple extract

Topping:
Mix together and pour over cake; return to oven and bake five minutes longer. Cool and refrigerate. It is better if baked the day before serving. May be frozen but allow 8 hours for thawing.

MRS. RODRIGUEZ'S CHEESECAKE WITH CRUST

1 pint sour cream
3 (8 ounce) packages
  cream cheese
1¼ cups sugar
6 eggs, separated
6 tablespoons flour
1 tablespoon lemon rind
1 tablespoon lemon juice
2 teaspoons vanilla

Mix all ingredients together in a large mixing bowl except egg whites. Beat until smooth. Beat egg whites until they form peaks. Fold into batter. Pour into graham cracker crust in springform pan. Bake at 350° for one hour and 15 minutes. Turn oven off and allow cake to cool in oven for 1 hour. Remove from oven and allow to cool to room temperature. Sprinkle with graham cracker crumbs from the following recipe. Refrigerate several hours or overnight before serving. Dust top of crumbs with powdered sugar.

Graham Cracker Crust:
1½ cups graham cracker
  crumbs
3 tablespoons sugar
¼ cup margarine, melted

Graham Cracker Crust:
Combine in a small bowl until well blended. Press 1 cup of crumb mixture into bottom and sides of buttered 9x3-inch springform pan. Chill while preparing filling. Save remaining crumb mixture to sprinkle on top of cake.

MRS. RODRIGUEZ'S CHEESECAKE WITHOUT CRUST

2 (8 ounce) packages
  cream cheese
1 pound creamed cottage
  cheese
1½ cups sugar
4 eggs, beaten
3 tablespoons cornstarch or
  flour
1½ tablespoons lemon
  juice
1 teaspoon lemon peel,
  grated
1 teaspoon vanilla
½ cup butter, melted
1 pint sour cream

Beat cheeses at high speed until well blended. Add eggs and sugar. Add remaining ingredients. Beat until smooth. Pour into greased springform pan. Bake at 325° for 1 hour and 10 minutes or until firm around edges. Turn oven off and leave in oven for 2 hours. Take out to cool. Put in refrigerator until thoroughly cool.

CHOCOLATE CHEESECAKE

Crust:
1¼ cups graham cracker
   crumbs
2 tablespoons sugar
3 tablespoons butter,
   melted
1 tablespoon cocoa

Crust:
Stir together graham cracker crumbs, sugar and cocoa; mix in butter until all crumbs are moistened. Press mixture evenly in bottom of ungreased 9-inch springform pan. Bake at 350° for 10 minutes. Cool completely. Reduce temperature of oven to 300°.

Filling:
2 (8 ounce) packages
   cream cheese
1 (3 ounce) package cream
   cheese
1 cup sugar
¼ cup cocoa
2 teaspoons vanilla
3 eggs

Filling:
Beat cream cheese in large mixer bowl. Gradually add sugar and cocoa, beating until fluffy. Add vanilla. Beat in eggs, one at a time. Pour mixture over crumb crust. Bake until center is firm, about 1 hour. Cool to room temperature. Spread Topping on top. Refrigerate at least 3 hours. Loosen edges of cheesecake with knife before removing side of pan.

Topping:
2 tablespoons butter or
   margarine
⅓ cup evaporated milk
2 tablespoons brown sugar
2 egg yolks
½ teaspoon vanilla
½ cup chopped pecans
½ cup flaked coconut

Topping:
Cook butter, milk, sugar and egg yolks in a small saucepan over low heat, stirring constantly, until thickened. Remove from heat. Stir in pecans and coconut. Cool slightly before spreading on cake.

PUMPKIN CHEESECAKE

20 ounce can crushed
  pineapple
16 ounce can pumpkin
1 cup brown sugar
3 eggs, beaten
1 teaspoon cinnamon
½ teaspoon ginger
1 envelope unflavored
  gelatin
2 (8 ounce) packages
  cream cheese
1 tablespoon vanilla
1 cup miniature
  marshmellows
½ cup whipping cream,
  whipped

Drain pineapple well, pressing out juice with back of spoon. Reserve ¾ cup juice. Cover pineapple and refrigerate. Combine juice with pumpkin, sugar, eggs, spices and gelatin in medium saucepan. Cover and simmer very slowly 30 minutes, stirring occasionally. Beat cream cheese and vanilla until fluffy. Gradually beat in warm pumpkin mixture until well blended. Pour into 8-inch graham cracker crust springform pan that has been baked at 350° for 10 minutes and cooled. Cover cheesecake and refrigerate overnight. Remove sides from pan and slide onto a serving plate. Fold pineapple and marshmellows into whipped cream. Spoon on top of cheesecake.

DADDY'S GRANDMA'S BROWN SUGAR FROSTING

¼ cup margarine
1 cup brown sugar
¼ cup milk
3¼ cups powdered sugar

Blend margarine and brown sugar, bring to a boil. Stir about one minute or until slightly thick. Cool slightly and add milk, beating until smooth. Beat in powdered sugar, enough for desired spreading consistency.

4-MINUTE BUTTER FROSTING

⅓ cup butter, softened
Pinch of salt
3 cups powdered sugar
¼ cup milk
1½ teaspoons vanilla

Cream butter, salt and 1 cup sugar until fluffy. Add remaining sugar and milk. Blend until smooth and spreading consistency. Add vanilla. Fills and frosts two 9-inch layers.

MOTHER'S BUTTERSCOTCH FROSTING

½ cup brown sugar,
  packed
6 tablespoons butter or
  shortening
⅓ cup milk
1½ cups powdered sugar
½ teaspooon vanilla
¼ teaspoon salt

Melt butter and brown sugar slowly. Add milk and boil for 2 minutes. Cool thoroughly. Add powdered sugar. Beat at high speed on mixer until thick enough to spread.

GRANDMA'S NUT CARAMEL ICING

1¼ cups brown sugar
⅓ cup water
¼ cup white sugar
2 eggs whites
1 teaspoon vanilla
¼ cup chopped nuts

Boil sugars and water until it threads (232°). Beat egg whites until stiff. Pour syrup very gradually into egg whites while beating. Continue beating until mixture is cool. Add vanilla and nuts.

RICH CHOCOLATE FROSTING

6 tablespoons butter
3 cups powdered sugar
1 teaspoon vanilla
Dash of salt
2½ squares unsweetened
   chocolate, melted OR
7 tablespoons cocoa
5 tablespoons milk, about

Cream butter. Add part of sugar. Mix in vanilla, salt and chocolate. Add remaining sugar and milk. Beat until smooth and desired spreading consistency.

COCONUT ICING

2½ cups sugar
½ cup corn syrup
¼ teaspoon salt
½ cup cold water
3 egg whites
1 teaspoon vanilla
12 large marshmellows
1 fresh coconut or 1 can of
   coconut

Boil sugar, syrup, salt and water until it forms a soft ball in cold water (236°). Beat egg whites until stiff, continue beating and pour syrup over egg whites very slowly. Add vanilla and marshmellows and continue beating until icing forms a peak when lifted with a spoon. Grate or grind coconut. Sprinkle over each layer as icing is spread on. Use this icing on a yellow or white cake.

FLOUR FROSTING

¼ cup flour
1 cup milk
Pinch of salt
½ cup shortening
1 cup sugar
1 stick margarine
1 teaspoon vanilla

Cook flour and milk over low heat, stirring until thick. Remove from heat, add salt and cool. Beat shortening, sugar and margarine until fluffy. Add flour mixture and vanilla; beat again. It will look like whipped cream. Frosts a 2 layer cake.

PEANUT BUTTER FROSTING - 1930'S

3 tablespoons butter
¼ cup peanut butter
1 teaspoon vanilla
¼ teaspoon salt
3 cups powdered sugar
5 tablespoons milk

Blend butter, peanut butter, vanilla and salt. Beat in ½ cup sugar. Add milk, alternately with remaining sugar, beating well after each addition. Add only enough milk to make a nice spreading consistency. Enough to frost tops and sides of two 8-inch layers.

SEA FOAM FROSTING

2 eggs
2 cups brown sugar
1 tablespoon white corn syrup
4 tablespoon cold water
1 teaspoon vanilla
Few grains of salt
¼ teaspoon cream of tartar

Beat all ingredients in top of a double boiler. Place over boiling water, use rotary beater or electric hand mixer and beat briskly until mixture will stand in peaks. Remove from over water, cool for a few minutes. Add vanilla and beat until cold. If too stiff add hot water by a teaspoon at a time and beat briskly. Ice any flavor of cake.

SEVEN MINUTE ICING

2 egg whites
1½ cups sugar
¼ teaspoon cream of tartar
⅓ cup water
¼ teaspoon salt
1 teaspoon vanilla

In top of a double boiler, before placing over heat, blend together egg whites, sugar, cream of tartar, water and salt. Beat the mixture for 2 minutes with an electric mixer. Place over boiling water and continue beating for 7 minutes more. Remove from heat and pan of water and add vanilla. Beat mixture 1 minute more. Ice any flavor of cake.

from Grandma's
Cookie Jar

GRANDMOTHER'S ANISE COOKIES (Springerle)

4 eggs
2¼ cups sugar
1 teaspoon lemon extract
4½ cups flour
1 teaspoon baking powder
1½ tablespoons anise seed
Anise Seed for top of
   cookies

Beat eggs; add sugar and mix well. Stir in lemon extract. Mix together flour and baking powder and add to egg mixture. Stir in the anise seed. Chill for 1 hour. Roll out ½ inch thick and cut in desired shape. Place on lightly greased cookie sheet and sprinkle a few anise seed on the top of each cookie. Bake at 350° for 20 minutes or until lightly golden. These are better after they age in an air tight container for several weeks.

BROWNIES (Cake-type)

1 cup shortening
4 squares unsweetened
   chocolate
4 eggs
2 cups sugar
½ teaspoon salt
2 teaspoons vanilla
1½ cups flour
1 teaspoon baking powder
1 cup chopped nuts

Melt shortening and chocolate together and cool. Beat eggs and add cooled melted shortening and chocolate; beat to a smooth cream. Add sugar, salt and vanilla. Mix in flour and baking powder. Blend together well. Stir in nuts. Turn into a buttered 9x13-inch pan. Bake at 325° for 35 to 40 minutes.

FUDGE-LIKE BROWNIES

1 cup butter or margarine
2 cups sugar
4 eggs
4 (1 ounce) squares
   unsweetened chocolate,
   melted
1 teaspoon vanilla
1 cup flour
½ teaspoon salt
1 cup pecans

Cream butter and sugar, add eggs and mix well. Add cooled, melted chocolate and vanilla. Add flour and salt. Mix well. Stir in pecans. Pour into a greased and floured 9x13-inch pan. Bake at 350° for 30 minutes.

CHOCOLATE CHOCOLATE CHIP BROWNIES

¾ cup flour
¼ teaspoon soda
¼ teaspoon salt
⅓ cup butter
¾ cup sugar
2 tablespoons water
1 (12 ounce) package
   chocolate chips
1 teaspoon vanilla
2 eggs
½ cup chopped nuts

Combine dry ingredients, set aside. In a small sauce pan combine butter, sugar and water; bring just to a boil. Remove from heat. Add 6 ounce (1 cup) of chocolate chips and vanilla. Stir until chips melt and mixture is smooth. Pour into a large mixing bowl. Add eggs, one at a time beating well after each. Blend in the dry ingredients. Stir in remaining chips and nuts. Spread into a greased 9-inch square pan. Bake at 325° for about 35 minutes. Cool completely before cutting into squares.

These are so good you may want to double the recipe and bake in a 9x13-inch pan!

DEBBIE'S BEST EVER BROWNIES

2 eggs
1 cup sugar
½ cup shortening or
   butter
2 squares unsweetened
   chocloate
½ cup flour
¼ teaspoon salt
1 teaspoon vanilla
1 cup old-fashioned
   oatmeal

Melt together shortening and chocolate. Cool slightly. Beat eggs; add sugar and remaining ingredients. Add chocolate mixture. Pour into greased 8x8-inch baking pan. Bake at 350° for 20 minutes.

CREAM CHEESE BROWNIES

1 (4 ounce) package
   German Sweet
   Chocolate
3 tablespoons butter
2 eggs
¾ cup sugar
½ teaspoon baking
   powder
¼ teaspoon salt
½ cup flour
1 teaspoon vanilla
¼ teaspoon almond
   extract
½ cup chopped nuts

Melt chocolate and butter over very low heat. Stir, then cool. Beat eggs until light colored. Slowly add sugar; beat until thickened. Add baking powder, salt and flour. Blend in chocolate mixture. Add vanilla, almond extract and nuts. Set aside while preparing the Cheese Layer.

Cheese Layer:
3 ounce package cream
   cheese
2 tablespoons butter
¼ cup sugar
1 egg
1 tablespoon flour
½ teaspoon vanilla

Cheese Layer:
Cream the cream cheese with butter. Gradually add sugar,; beat until fluffy. Blend in egg, flour and vanilla.

Spread half of the chocolate batter in a greased 8 or 9-inch square pan. Top with the cheese mixture. Spoon remaining chocolate batter over top. Zigzag knife through the batter to marble. Bake at 350° for 35 to 40 minutes. Cool before cutting.

EASY AND DELICIOUS BROWNIES

2 cups sugar
4 eggs
1 cup oil
3 to 4 tablespoons cocoa
1 teaspoon vanilla
1½ cups flour
1 teaspoon baking powder
½ teaspoon salt
1 cup chopped pecans

Cream sugar and eggs. Add oil, cocoa and vanilla. Sift together flour, baking powder and salt. Add to egg mixture. Mix well. Add pecans. Pour into a 9x13-inch pan that has been greased and floured. Bake at 350° for 30 to 35 minutes. Avoid over-baking.

GRANDMOTHER'S FUDGEY BROWNIES

¾ cup cocoa
½ teaspoon soda
⅔ cup oil
½ cup boiling water
2 cups sugar
2 eggs
1½ cups flour
¼ teaspoon salt
1 teaspoon vanilla
½ cup chopped pecans

Stir cocoa and soda in mixing bowl. Blend in ⅓ cup oil. Add boiling water; stir until mixture thickens. Stir in sugar, eggs and remaining ⅓ cup oil. Stir until smooth. Add flour, salt and vanilla, blend completely. Stir in nuts. Pour into a lightly greased 9x13 inch pan. Bake at 350° for 35 to 40 minutes. Cool. Frost, if desired.

CARAMEL BROWNIES

⅔ cup evaporated milk
14 ounce bag of caramels
1 German Chocolate Cake Mix
1½ sticks margarine, melted
12 ounce bag of chocolate chips

In a double boiler melt caramels with ⅓ cup of milk. Mix together cake mix, margarine and ⅓ cup of milk. Pat ½ of this into a 9x13-inch pan. Bake at 350° for 7 minutes. Let cool, then pour melted caramels on top. Cover with chocolate chips, then cover with remaining cake mixture. Bake at 350° for about 18 to 20 minutes. Cut into squares. These are very rich so cut into small squares.

DROP BROWNIES

½ cup butter or
 margarine
1 cup sugar
2 eggs, beaten
1½ teaspoons vanilla
2 (1 ounce) squares
 unsweetened chocolate
 melted
1 cup flour
½ teaspoon baking
 powder
¾ teaspoon salt
3 cups chopped pecans

Cream butter and sugar. Add eggs, vanilla, melted chocolate and blend well. Sift dry ingredients together and stir into creamed mixture. Add nuts. Drop by teaspoon on lightly greased cookie sheet. Bake at 350° for 10 minutes.

BLACK FOREST COOKIES

½ cup margarine or
 butter, softened
1 cup sugar
1 egg
1 teaspoon vanilla
1½ cups flour
½ cup cocoa
¼ teaspoon salt
¼ teaspoon baking
 powder
¼ teaspoon soda
10 ounce jar maraschino
 cherries

In a large bowl, cream margarine, sugar, egg and vanilla until light and fluffy. Add remaining ingredients except cherries, and blend at low speed about 1 minute. Shape dough into 1 inch balls. Place on an ungreased cookie sheet about 2 inches apart. Push one whole cherry halfway into each ball. When all cookies are formed, make the frosting and use immediately. Yes, you frost the cookies before you bake them.

Frosting:
6 ounce package
 semi-sweet chocolate
 chips
½ cup sweetened
 condensed milk
¼ teaspoon salt
1½ teaspoons cherry
 juice

Frosting:
In a small saucepan, melt chocolate and milk over low heat, stirring constantly. Remove from heat. Add salt and juice, stir until smooth. Frost each cherry with ½ teaspoon of frosting. Bake frosted cookies at 350° for 8 to 10 minutes.

CHOCOROONS

1½ cups flour
⅔ cup Nestle's Quik
  Chocolate Mix
1½ teaspoons baking
  powder
¼ teaspoon salt
½ cup butter
¼ cup sugar
2 egg yolks
1 tablespoon milk
½ teaspoon vanilla

Cream butter and sugar; add egg yolks, milk and vanilla; beat well. Blend in dry ingredients and mix well. Chill. Roll out dough ¼ inch thick on a lightly floured board; cut with a biscuit cutter. On half of the circles place a spoonful of Coconut Filling and cover with another circle of dough, press around the edges with a fork to seal. Place on ungreased cookie sheet. Bake at 325° for 12 to 15 minutes. Cool. Frost top with Frosting.

Coconut Filling:
Beat 2 egg whites, 1 teaspoon almond extract, ½ teaspoon vanilla, until soft mounds form. Gradually add ¼ cup sugar; beat until stiff peaks form. Fold in 7 ounce package grated coconut and 1 tablespoon water.

Chocolate Frosting:
Combine 1 cup Nestle's Quik Chocolate Mix, ¼ cup butter and ¼ cup boiling water. Blend in 2¼ cups sifted powdered sugar, 1 teaspoon vanilla. Beat until thick. If necessary thin with milk.

These may appear to be a lot of trouble to make, but they are not difficult and well worth the time. Kids love them!

DEBBIE'S CHOCOLATE NO BAKES

2 cups sugar
4 tablespoons cocoa
½ cup margarine
½ cup milk
1 teaspoon vanilla
½ cup peanut butter
3 cups uncooked oatmeal

Combine first 4 ingredients in a sauce pan and bring to boil. Boil hard for 2 minutes. Remove from fire. Add remaining ingredients. Mix well, work fast, drop by teaspoon onto wax paper. Let stand until cookies are well set.

CHEWY CHOCOLATE COOKIES

1¼ cups margarine
2 cups sugar
2 eggs
2 teaspoons vanilla
2 cups flour
¾ cup cocoa
1 teaspoon soda
½ teaspoon salt
1 cup finely chopped nuts

Cream butter and sugar; add eggs and vanilla. Combine dry ingredients and combine with egg mixture. Stir in nuts, if desired. Drop by teaspoonfuls on an ungreased cookie sheet. Bake at 350° for 8 to 10 minutes. DO NOT OVER BAKE! Cookies will be soft and puff while baking, they will flatten while cooling. Cool about one minute on the cookie sheet until set. Remove to a wire rack and allow to cool thoroughly.

CHOCOLATE-CHOCOLATE MINT COOKIES

¾ cup firmly packed
  brown sugar
½ cup sugar
1 cup margarine, softened
1 teaspoon vanilla
1 egg
1¾ cups flour
¼ cup cocoa
1 teaspoon soda
½ teaspoon salt
6 ounces (1 cup) chocolate
  mint chips
½ cup chopped nuts

Cream sugars and margarine until light and fluffy; blend in vanilla and egg. Blend flour, cocoa, soda and salt into creamed mixture. Stir in chips and nuts. Drop dough by spoonfuls onto ungreased cookie sheet. Bake at 375° for 7 to 10 minutes.

CHOC-CO-NUT SQUARES

1½ cups butter or
   margarine
1½ cups brown sugar,
   packed
1 teaspoon vanilla
1 teaspoon butter flavoring
3 cups flour
1 (12 ounce) package
   chocolate chips
1 cup chopped nuts
1 cup grated coconut

Cream butter, sugar, vanilla and butter flavoring. Add flour, mix well. Stir in chocolate chips, nuts and coconut. Press into ungreased 9x13-inch pan. Bake at 325° for 25 minutes. While warm cut into squares. Cool before removing from pan.

AUNT LOUISE'S FAMOUS NAMELESS COOKIES

⅔ cup oil
1 pound margarine
1 pound brown sugar
2 cups sugar
4 eggs, well beaten
2 teaspoons baking powder
½ teaspoon salt
1 teaspoon vanilla
7 cups flour
12 ounce package
   butterscotch chips
6 ounces chocolate chips
1 teaspoon coconut extract
1 cup coconut
1 cup pecans

Cream oil, margarine and sugars. Add remaining ingredients in order given, working in well until dough no longer sticks to hands. Drop by Tablespoon onto ungreased cookie sheet. Bake at 350° for 10 to 12 minutes. Remove to waxed paper lined surface to cool for 10 minutes before storing.

(Bake one cookie sheet at a time or the cookies on the outer edge of sheet will bake before those in center.)
(These freeze well - the unbaked dough or the baked cookies.)

BUFFALO CHIPO'S

2 cups shortening or butter
2 cups brown sugar
2 cups granulated sugar
4 large eggs
2 tablespoons vanilla
4 cups flour
2 teaspoons soda
2 teaspoons baking powder
½ teaspoon salt
2 cups old-fashioned oats
3 cups cornflakes
1 cup chopped pecans
1 cup coconut
1 (12 ounce) package
  chocolate chips
1 (12 ounce) package milk
  chocolate chips
1 (6 ounce) package
  butterscotch chips

Cream together first 5 ingredients until smooth. Mix together the flour, soda, baking powder and salt; add to sugar mixture. Add the remaining ingredients in the order given. Mix well. Drop by tablespoon onto cookie sheet and bake at 350° until golden brown.

These are big cookies--the size of a buffalo chip!

DAVID'S FAVORITE DOLLIES

1 stick margarine, softened
1½ cups graham cracker
  crumbs
1 (6 ounce) package
  chocolate chips
1 (3½ ounce) can flaked
  coconut
1 cup chopped nuts
14 ounce can sweetened
  condensed milk

Mix margarine and crumbs, press into a 9x13-inch pan. Sprinkle with chocolate chips; then coconut; then nuts. Pour milk over the top. Bake at 350° for 25 to 30 minutes or until browned. Cool. Cut into squares.

COCONUT PECAN BAR COOKIES

1¼ cups flour
⅛ teaspoon salt
1¼ cups brown sugar, packed
⅓ cup melted butter
2 eggs
½ teaspoon baking powder
½ teaspoon almond extract
½ teaspoon vanilla
1¼ cups flaked coconut
1 cup chopped pecans

Mix together 1 cup of flour, salt and ¼ cup of sugar. Add melted butter and mix until smooth. Press the mixture into the bottom of a lightly greased 8-inch square pan. Bake for 15 minutes at 350°. Prepare the topping while this is cooking. Beat eggs well, then gradually beat in remaining sugar, beat together until fluffy. Sift together flour and baking powder. Add to creamed mixture and beat well. Add extracts, coconut and nuts. Spread mixture quickly over the baked pastry. Return it to the oven and bake for 20 minutes or until browned. Leave in pan to cool. Cut into squares.

COCONUT MACAROONS

2⅔ cups coconut
¾ cup sweetened condensed milk
1 egg, beaten
¼ teaspoon almond extract
1 teaspoon vanilla

Combine all ingredients. Let stand 2 to 3 minutes. Drop on greased cookie sheet. Flatten slightly. Bake at 300° for about 25 minutes.

COWBOY COOKIES

1 cup shortening
1 cup sugar
1 cup brown sugar
2 eggs
2 cups flour
½ teaspoon baking powder
1 teaspoon cinnamon
1 teaspoon soda
½ teaspoon salt
2 cups old-fashioned oats
1 teaspoon vanilla
1 cup raisins
1 cup chopped pecans
1 cup coconut
1 (6 ounce) package
  chocolate chips

Blend shortening and sugars. Beat in eggs. Stir in flour, cinnamon, baking powder, soda and salt. Mix in vanilla. Add remaining ingredients and mix well. Drop onto greased cookie sheets and bake at 350° for 15 minutes.

ALMOND CRESCENT COOKIES

1 (10 ounce) package or 2
  cups whole almonds
1¼ cups flour
¼ cup sugar
1 cup butter
1 teaspoon vanilla
Powdered sugar

Whirl almonds in blender or grind fine. Mix flour, sugar and almonds. With fingers work in butter and vanilla until mixture leaves the bowl. Chill about 1 hour. Roll dough into balls then into rolls and form into crescents. Bake on ungreased cookie sheet at 350° for about 12 to 15 minutes or until lightly browned. Cool in pan about 10 minutes. While still warm roll in powdered sugar. Makes about 25 cookies.

DATE OATMEAL SQUARES

Filling:
1 cup (8 ounce) chopped
  dates
¼ cup brown sugar
¼ cup chopped pecans
4 teaspoons lemon juice
⅓ cup water
1 teaspoon vanilla

Crumb Mixture:
½ cup margarine, softened
1 cup brown sugar, packed
3 cups rolled oats
½ teaspoon cinnamon

Mix together filling ingredients in a saucepan and cook over low heat until soft. Cream margarine and brown sugar. Mix in oats and cinnamon until well blended. Press half of crumb mixture into a greased 9-inch square pan. Spread date mixture over crumbs then sprinkle with remaining crumb mixture. Press lightly. Bake at 375° for 30 minutes or until lightly browned. Cut into squares while warm. Cool before removing from pan.

DEBBIE'S FRUIT BARS

¾ cup margarine
1 cup brown sugar
1½ cups flour
1 teaspoon salt
½ teaspoon soda
1½ cups old-fashioned or
  quick oats
1 can cherry pie filling or
  10 ounce jar preserves

Cream margarine and sugar until light and fluffy. Add combined dry ingredients; mix well. Press half of crumb mixture into greased 9x13-inch pan. Spread with pie filling or preserves; sprinkle with remaining crumb mixture. Bake at 400° for 20 to 25 minutes. Cool; cut into bars.

(Sometimes it is necessary to increase crumb mixture so you will have more on the top.)

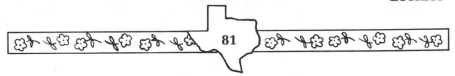
FRUITCAKE COOKIES

1 pound dates
¾ pound candied cherries
¾ pound candied
  pineapple
½ pound raisins
1 cup Bourbon or wine
½ cup butter
1 cup sugar
½ cup brown sugar
4 eggs
1 teaspoon cinnamon
1 teaspoon nutmeg
1 teaspoon allspice
4 cups flour
3 teaspoons baking soda
  dissolved in
3 tablespoons milk
1 to 1½ pounds pecans

Cut up dates, cherries and pineapple. Add raisins and soak overnight in bourbon or wine. Cream butter and sugars. Add eggs and beat well. Sift spices with flour. Alternately add flour mixture with milk and soda mixture. Fold in fruits and nuts. Drop by spoonful on greased cookie sheet. Bake at 300° for 15 minutes.

Makes a very large batch. Store in air tight container to keep soft and fresh. They are best after about a week.

LITTLE FUDGE TARTS

1½ cups flour
¼ teaspoon salt
½ cup margarine, softened
3 tablespoons water
1 teaspoon vanilla

Filling:
¼ cup margarine, softened
1 egg yolk
½ cup sugar
1 teaspoon vanilla
¼ cup cocoa
½ cup finely chopped nuts

Mix together flour and salt, with a fork cut in margarine. Sprinkle with water and vanilla and mix with fork. Roll out ½ of dough at a time on a lightly floured surface 1/16 inch thick. Cut into 2½ inch squares. Mix together all filling ingredients. Put a teaspoon of the filling in the center of each square. Bring corners to center and seal together. Place on ungreased baking sheet. Bake at 350° for 15 to 20 minutes.

CRISP GINGERSNAPS (200 yr. old recipe)

2 cups medium heavy cane
   syrup
1 cup butter
¼ teaspoon salt
1 tablespoon ground ginger
2 teaspoons soda
5½ cups flour (or enough
   to make a soft dough)

Boil together syrup, butter, salt and ginger. Let boil 2 minutes or longer if syrup is thin. Set aside to cool. Add soda and beat thoroughly. Add flour to make dough as soft as can be handled. Roll out to about ⅛ inch thick. Cut and bake on a greased cookie sheet at 300° until done. These burn easily!

GRANDMA'S GINGERSNAPS

1 cup margarine, melted
1 cup sugar
¼ cup molasses
1 egg
2 cups flour
1 teaspoon soda
½ teaspoon ground cloves
1½ teaspoons ginger
1 teaspoon cinnamon
½ teaspoon salt

Cool margarine and mix with sugar, molasses and egg; mix well. Sift together dry ingredients and add to sugar mixture. Mix well. Cover and chill for at least 2 hours. Roll into walnut size balls, then roll each in granulated sugar. Place on greased cookie sheet leaving space to spread. Bake at 375° for 8 to 10 minutes. Watch close, they brown quickly on the bottom. Remove from pans immediately and cool on wire racks.

JELLO COOKIES

1½ cups butter or
   margaine
1 cup sugar
1 (3 ounce) package Jello,
   any flavor
1 egg
1 teaspoon vanilla
4 cups flour
1 teaspoon baking powder

Cream butter, add sugar and Jello. Mix in egg and vanilla. Gradually add flour and baking powder, mix well. Chill and then roll out and cut. Bake on lightly greased cookie sheet at 400° until slightly golden around the edges.

CREAM CHEESE LEMON BARS

Crust:
1 cup flour
⅓ cup sugar
2 teaspoons lemon peel
¼ cup butter, softened
2 ounces cream cheese,
  softened

Crust:
Combine ingredients for crust. Blend with mixer until particles are fine. Press into well greased 9x13-inch pan. Bake at 350° for 12 to 15 minutes or until light brown.

Filling
6 ounces cream cheese,
  softened
⅓ cup sugar
2 eggs
1 teaspoon lemon peel
2 tablespoons lemon juice

Filling:
Combine ingredients for Filling in a small mixer bowl. Blend well. Pour filling over partially baked crust.

Topping:
2 tablespoons flour
1 teaspoon baking powder
½ teaspoon salt
1 cup brown sugar, packed
2 eggs
1 teaspoon vanilla
1 cup chopped nuts

Topping:
Combine ingredients for Topping in a small mixer bowl except nuts. Blend well. Stir in ¾ cup nuts. Spoon Topping over filling and sprinkle with ¼ cup nuts. Bake at 350° for 25 to 30 minutes. Cool; cut into bars.

LEMON CHEESE PRESSED COOKIES

1 cup butter or margarine
3 ounces cream cheese
1 cup sugar
1 egg, beaten
1 tablespoon lemon juice
1 teaspoon grated lemon
  peel
2½ cups flour
1 teaspoon baking powder
1 teaspoon lemon extract

Blend butter and cream cheese. Add sugar; cream thoroughly. Add egg, lemon juice, peel and extract; blend well. Blend in flour and baking powder; mix thoroughly. Chill dough 30 minutes. Press dough out of cookie press onto an ungreased cookie sheet. Bake at 375° for 8 to 10 minutes or until slightly browned. Makes about 5 dozen.

LEMONY CHEESECAKE COOKIE SQUARES

⅓ cup brown sugar,
  packed
½ cup walnuts, chopped
1 cup flour
⅓ cup butter, melted
1 (8 ounce) package cream
  cheese
¼ cup sugar
1 egg
1 tablespoon lemon juice
2 tablespoons milk
1 teaspoon vanilla

Mix brown sugar, nuts and flour together in a large bowl. Stir in melted butter and mix with your hands until light and crumbly. Remove 1 cup of the mixture to be used later as a topping. Place remainder in an 8-inch square pan and press firmly. Bake at 350° for about 12 to 15 minutes. While this is baking, beat cream cheese until smooth with the ¼ cup of sugar. Beat in the egg, lemon juice, milk and vanilla. Pour this onto the baked crust. Top with the reserved crumbs. Return to a 350° oven and bake for about 25 minutes. Cool thoroughly, then cut into 2-inch squares.

LEMONY LEMON SQUARES

Crust:
1 cup butter, softened
½ cup powdered sugar
2 cups flour
Pinch of salt

Combine crust ingredients; blend thoroughly. Pat evenly into a 10x15-inch pan. Bake at 350° for 20 minutes.

Topping:
4 eggs
2 cups sugar
6 tablespoons flour
½ teaspoon baking powder
6 tablespoons fresh lemon
  juice
3 tablespoons lemon rind
Confectioners' sugar

Topping:
Beat eggs slightly; stir in sugar, flour, baking powder, lemon juice and rind. Mix well and spread over baked crust. Bake at 350° for 25 minutes. When done sprinkle with confectioners' sugar.

LEMON SHORTBREAD

4 cups flour
½ teaspoon baking powder
2 cups butter, softened
1 cup powdered sugar,
  sifted
Rind of 4 lemons, finely
  grated
2 teaspoons lemon extract

Cream butter; slowly add sugar beating well between additions. Blend in the rind and extract. Beat in the flour and baking powder, beating just until the flour particles are moistened.

Roll out about ½ inch thick. Place the uncut dough on a cookie sheet and refrigerate for at least 5 hours. Cut out cookies and place them on paper-lined cookie sheet. Pierce the top several times with a fork. Bake at 350° for about 10 to 15 minutes or until firm to the touch.

M & M COOKIES

1 cup shortening
1 cup brown sugar
½ cup sugar
2 teaspoons vanilla
2 eggs
2½ cups flour
1 teaspoon soda
1 teaspoon salt
1½ cups M&M's

Cream shortening and sugars. Beat in vanilla and eggs. Sift together dry ingredients; add to creamed mixture. Mix well. Stir in ½ cup of candy - reserve remaining candy for decorating. Drop from teaspoon on ungreased cookie sheet, decorate tops with candy. Bake at 375° for about 10 minutes or until golden brown.

SURPRISE MERINGUE KISSES

3 egg whites, room
  temperature
1 teaspoon vanilla
¼ teaspoon cream of tartar
¼ teaspoon peppermint
  extract
Dash of salt
1 cup sugar
44 milk chocolate kisses
Green sugar crystals

In a small mixer bowl sprinkle cream of tartar and salt on egg whites and beat to soft peaks, about 1 minute. Add vanilla and peppermint extract. Continue beating at high speed and gradually add sugar, about 1 tablespoon at a time. Beat to very stiff peaks, about 7 minutes. Drop from a tablespoon 1½ inch apart onto a lightly greased cookie sheet. Press a chocolate kiss into each mound. With a knife bring meringue up and over candy, swirl the top. Sprinkle with green sugar. Bake at 275° for 30 minutes or until set. Immediately remove cookies to a rack. Cool.

AUNT ALICE'S OATMEAL COOKIES

¾ cup shortening or
  margarine
1 cup brown sugar
½ cup sugar
1 egg
1 teaspoon vanilla
¼ cup water
1¼ cups flour
1 teaspoon salt
½ teaspoon soda
3 cups oatmeal
1 cup raisins or nuts or
  chocolate chips

Combine first 6 ingredients. Mix together flour, salt and soda. Add oatmeal and any of the last ingredients. Bake at 350° on greased cookie sheet.

SUZIE'S OATMEAL CARAMEL BARS

Crust and Topping:
2 cups flour
2 cups quick-cooking oats
1½ cups brown sugar,
   packed
1 teaspoon soda
½ teaspoon salt
1¼ cups margarine,
   softened

Filling:
6 ounce package chocolate
   chips
½ cup chopped nuts
12 ounce jar caramel ice
   cream topping
3 tablespoons flour

Combine crust ingredients, blend to form crumbs. Press half of crumbs (about 3 cups) into greased 9x13-inch pan. Bake 10 minutes at 350°. Sprinkle with chocolate chips and nuts. Blend caramel topping and flour; drizzle over chocolate chips and nuts. Sprinkle with remaining crumbs. Return to oven; bake 18 to 22 minutes, until golden brown. Cool completely before cutting into bars. Chilling will make cutting easier.

BUTTERSCOTCH OATMEAL COOKIES

1 cup butter
1½ cups brown sugar,
   packed
2 eggs
1 tablespoon water
2 cups flour
2 teaspoons baking powder
1 teaspoon soda
1 teaspoon salt
1¾ cups quick oats
12 ounce package
   butterscotch chips
½ teaspoon orange extract

Combine butter, brown sugar, eggs and water; beat until creamy. Gradually add flour, baking powder, soda and salt which have been combined. Stir in oats, chips and extract. Drop by spoonfuls onto greased cookie sheet. Bake at 375° for 10 to 12 minutes.

GREAT OATMEAL CHIP COOKIES

2 cups flour
1 teaspoon salt
1 teaspoon soda
1 cup sugar
1 cup brown sugar, packed
½ cup margarine, softened
½ cup shortening
2 eggs
2 cups quick oatmeal
1 cup nuts, chopped
1 cup (6 ounce) package
   chocolate chips

Combine all ingredients except for last three. Blend well with mixer. Stir in last three ingredients and mix thoroughly. Chill dough. Roll into 1 ounce balls. Bake on ungreased cookie sheet. Bake at 375° for about 10 to 12 minutes. Cool on wire racks.

MRS. GOODMAN'S OATMEAL COOKIES

1 cup shortening
½ cup sugar
1 cup brown sugar
3 eggs
1 cup flour
2 teaspoons baking powder
½ teaspoon soda
½ teaspoon salt
3 cups old-fashioned
   oatmeal
1 cup raisins
1 cup nuts, chopped

Cream shortening and sugars. Add eggs. Add dry ingredients, then oatmeal one cup at a time. Add nuts and raisins. Drop on greased cookie sheet, allow room for spreading. Bake at 350° for about 12 to 14 minutes.

GRANDMOTHER'S OATMEAL MACAROONS

1 cup shortening
1 cup brown sugar, firmly
  packed
1 cup white sugar
1 teaspoon vanilla
½ teaspoon cinnamon
2 eggs
1¼ cups flour
1 teaspoon soda
½ teaspoon salt
3 cups oatmeal
½ cup chopped nuts
  and/or
1 cup raisins
1 cup coconut
1 cup chocolate chips
1 cup butterscotch chips

Cream shortening and sugars; add vanilla. Add eggs and beat until fluffy. Thoroughly blend in dry ingredients which have been sifted together. Mix in oatmeal about 1 cup at a time. Stir in nuts and /or raisins, coconut or chips. Drop by spoon on ungreased cookie sheet. Bake at 350° for about 15 minutes.

GRANDMA'S OATMEAL COOKIES (From the early 1920's)

½ cup sugar
½ cup butter
1 egg
½ teaspoon vanilla
½ teaspoon salt
½ teaspoon soda
½ cup raisins or chopped
  dates
½ cup chopped nuts
1 cup flour
1½ cups oatmeal

Cream sugar and butter. Add egg, beat till fluffy. Add vanilla. Mix together flour, salt and soda; add to egg mixture. Slowly mix in oatmeal. Stir in raisins and nuts. Bake at 350° on a greased cookie sheet until done.

GREAT OATMEAL COOKIES

2 cups flour
1 cup sugar
1 cup brown sugar
1 teaspoon baking powder
1 teaspoon soda
½ teaspoon salt
1 cup shortening
2 eggs
1 teaspoon vanilla
1½ cups quick cooking
  oats
½ cup chopped nuts
Sugar & cinnamon

Mix together first 6 ingredients. Add shortneing, eggs and vanilla; beat well. Stir in oats and nuts. Form into small balls. Place on ungreased cookie sheet; flatten with the bottom of a glass that has been oiled and dipped in sugar-cinnamon mixture. Bake at 350° for about 10 minutes.

QUICK AND TASTY OATMEAL COOKIES

1½ cups flour
1 cup sugar
1 cup brown sugar, packed
1 teaspoon salt
1 teaspoon soda
1 cup shortening or
  margarine
1 teaspoon vanilla
2 eggs
3 cups rolled oats

Combine all ingredients except oats, beat 1 minute at medium speed. Stir in oats. Drop on un-greased cookie sheet about 2 inches apart. Bake at 350° for about 12 minutes. Cool slightly before removing from cookie sheet.

CHOCOLATE OATMEAL COOKIES

1 cup shortening
1½ cups sugar
2 eggs
¾ teaspoon soda
½ teaspoon salt
1½ cups flour
1 teaspoon cinnamon
3 cups oatmeal
1 cup chopped nuts
2 tablespoons cocoa
1 teaspoon vanilla

Cream shortening and sugar. Add eggs. Mix together the soda, salt, flour and cinnamon; add to sugar mixture. Add remaining ingredients in the order given. Drop by spoonfuls onto cookie sheet. Bake at 350° for about 18 minutes.

SOFT OATMEAL RAISIN COOKIES

⅔ cup shortening
1 cup sugar
2 eggs, beaten
1½ cups flour
½ teaspoon soda
½ teaspoon salt
2 teaspoons cinnamon
½ cup milk
1½ cups old-fashioned
  oatmeal
1 cup raisins
½ cup chopped nuts

Cream shortening and sugar, then beat in eggs. Add dry ingredients alternately with milk. Mix well. Stir in oatmeal, raisins and nuts. Drop onto greased cookie sheet and bake at 400° for about 15 minutes.

GRANDMA'S ORANGE COOKIES

1 cup sugar
½ cup shortening
1 egg
½ teaspoon vanilla
2 teaspoons orange extract
1 teaspoon butter flavoring
2 cups flour
¼ teaspoon salt
2 tablespoons milk
½ teaspoon soda

Cream sugar and shortening. Add egg and flavorings; mix well. Sift together dry ingredients and mix into sugar mixture. Stir in milk.

Dip hands in flour and form dough into small balls, place on greased cookie sheet 2 inches apart. Flatten with the bottom of a glass that has a small amount of oil on it and then dipped into sugar before pressing each cookie. Bake at 400° for about 10 minutes or until edges are golden.

ORANGE SLICE BARS

2 cups brown sugar
½ cup shortening
3 eggs, beaten
2 cups flour
½ teaspoon baking powder
½ teaspoon salt
1 teaspoon soda
2 cups (1 pound) candy
　orange slices, chopped
1 cup chopped nuts
1 teaspoon cinnamon

Cream sugar and shortening. Add eggs. Mix together dry ingredients and add. Fold in chopped candy and nuts. Spoon into a greased 9x13-inch pan and bake at 325° for 30 minutes.

ORANGE SLICE COOKIES

1 cup sugar
1 cup brown sugar
1 cup shortening
2 eggs
1 teaspoon vanilla
2 cups flour
1 teaspoon baking powder
1 teaspoon soda
½ teaspoon salt
2 cups quick-cooking oats
2 cups (12 ounce) candy
　orange slices, sliced
1 cup flaked coconut

Cream sugars and shortening until fluffy. Add eggs and vanilla; beat well. Stir together dry ingredients. Stir into creamed mixture. Stir in oats, candy and coconut. Roll about a tablespoon of the mixture into balls. Place on greased cookie sheet. Bake at 350° for about 10 minutes or till lightly browned. Remove and cool on a wire rack.

PEANUTTY BARS

Crust:
1 cup (2 sticks) margarine
¾ cup sugar
1 egg
1 teaspoon vanilla
2½ cups flour

Crust:
Cream margarine and sugar for crust until fluffy. Add egg and vanilla. Gradually add flour, blend well. Press into the bottom of a buttered 9x13-inch pan. Bake about 10 minutes, until slightly brown.

Topping:
4 ounces sweet or
  semi-sweet chocolate
¼ cup margarine
1 cup powdered sugar,
  sifted
1 egg, slightly beaten
6 ounces miniature
  marshmellows
1 cup salted peanuts

Topping:
For the topping, melt the chocolate and margarine in a saucepan, stir until smooth; remove from heat. Stir in sifted powdered sugar, add egg and beat until smooth. Fold in marshmellows and peanuts to slightly cooled chocolate mixture. Spread over the cooked dough. Chill before cutting into bars. Keeps well in the refrigerator.

PEANUT BUTTER COOKIES

3 cups flour
2 teaspoons baking powder
¼ teaspoon salt
1 cup butter
1 cup sugar
1 cup brown sugar, firmly
  packed
2 eggs, well-beaten
1 cup peanut butter
½ teaspoon vanilla

Sift together flour, baking powder and salt. Cream together butter and sugars. Add eggs and mix until smooth. Add peanut butter and vanilla; stir well. Thoroughly blend in dry ingredients. Dough will be stiff. Form dough into walnut size balls; place on greased baking sheet. Press each ball the a fork to make a waffle design. Bake at 375° for 10 to 12 minutes. Make about 5 dozen.

PECAN TASSIES
(Little Pecan Pie)

6 ounces cream cheese,
 softened
1 cup butter, softened
2 cups flour
3 eggs
2¼ cups brown sugar
3 tablespoons butter,
 softened
3 teaspoons vanilla
Dash of salt
2 cups pecan pieces

Blend together cream cheese and butter. Add flour and blend in well. Chill slightly. Form into balls, depending on the size of muffin tins used. Press dough evenly in ungreased muffin tins. Beat eggs, sugar, butter, vanilla and salt until smooth. Spoon mixture into each muffin tin lined with dough. Top with pecans. Bake at 350° for about 25 to 30 minutes for the regular muffin tin size. Cool before removing from tins.

TEXAS PECAN BARS

Crust:
1⅓ cups flour
½ cup brown sugar,
 packed
¼ teaspoon baking powder
⅓ cup butter, softened

Topping:
1 cup corn syrup
1 cup brown sugar, packed
2 tablespoons flour
½ teaspoon salt
3 eggs
1 teaspoon vanilla
¾ cup chopped pecans

Combine crust ingredients, blend with mixer until particles are fine. Press into a greased 9x13-inch pan. Combine topping ingredients except for pecans. Blend well. Pour over crust. Sprinkle with pecans. Bake at 350° for 25 to 30 minutes. Cool, cut into bars.

These are great! They are like pecan pie.

PECAN SHORTBREAD COOKIES

2 cups flour
¼ teaspoon baking powder
1 cup butter or margarine
½ cup powdered sugar
½ cup finely chopped nuts

Sift flour with baking powder. Cream butter with powdered sugar until light and fluffy. Gradually blend in flour mixture. Stir in nuts. Cover and chill. Roll out on lightly floured board to ¼ inch thick and cut into desired shapes. Place on an ungreased cookie sheet. Bake at 300° for about 20 minutes or until edges are lightly browned. Cool on wire rack.

PECAN TURTLE COOKIE BARS

Crust:
2 cups flour
1 cup brown sugar, packed
½ cup butter, softened

Topping:
⅔ cup butter
½ cup brown sugar, packed
1 cup whole pecans
1 cup milk chocolate chips

Combine crust ingredients, mix well until particles are fine. Pat firmly into an ungreased 9x13-inch pan. Sprinkle pecans evenly over unbaked crust. Combine brown sugar and butter. Cook over medium heat, stirring constantly, until mixture begins to boil. Boil for about 1 minute, continue to stir. Pour over pecans and crust. Bake at 350° for 18 to 22 minutes or until entire layer of caramel is bubbly and crust is light brown. Remove from oven and sprinkle with chocolate chips. Allow chips to melt and slightly swirl as they melt, leave some whole. Cool completely before cutting into squares.

PINEAPPLE CHEESECAKE BARS

Base:
1 cup flour
½ cup sugar
½ cup margarine, softened

Filling:
2 tablespoons sugar
8 ounce package cream cheese
2 tablespoons milk
1 teaspoon vanilla
1 egg
20 ounce can crushed pineapple (well drained)

Stir together all base ingredients until crumbs form. Press in bottom of ungreased 9x13-inch pan. Bake at 350° for 10 to 15 minutes or until lightly browned. Beat together sugar, cream cheese, milk, vanilla and egg at medium speed for 3 minutes until smooth. Stir in drained pineapple. Pour over partially baked crust.

Topping:
1 cup coconut
1 tablespoon margarine, melted

Topping:
Combine coconut and melted margarine and sprinkle over filling. Return to oven and bake 15 to 20 minutes or until filling is set and coconut is golden brown. Cool completely. Cut into bars. Store in refrigerator.

DADDY'S GRANDMA'S PINEAPPLE COOKIES

⅔ cup shortening
1½ cups sugar
2 eggs, well beaten
4 tablespoons pineapple juice
1 tablespoon hot water
1 teaspoon vanilla
3 cups flour
½ teaspoon soda
1 small can pineapple, cut into small pieces

Cream shortening; beat in sugar, eggs, vanilla, juice and water. Mix well. Stir soda into flour and mix into batter. Drop by teaspoon onto ungreased cookie sheet. Place a small piece of the pineapple on top of each cookie. Bake at 300° until edges are golden.

MR. HOLMES RUSSIAN ROCK COOKIES

1 cup butter or shortening
1¾ cups dark brown sugar, packed
3 eggs
3 cups flour
½ teaspoon salt
1½ teaspoons cinnamon
1 pound raisins
1 cup chopped nuts
1 teaspoon soda
1 tablespoon water

Cream butter and sugar. Add eggs, flour, salt and cinnamon. Stir in raisins and nuts. Dissolve soda in water and add. Drop by teaspoon on cookie sheet about 1 inch apart. Bake at 375° for 8 to 10 minutes. Check after 5 minutes for browness.

Butter makes cookies a little moist and chewy. Shortening makes them more crisp.

WWI SOUTHERN ROCKS

1 cup butter, softened
1½ cups sugar
3 eggs, separated
1 teaspoon vanilla
3 cups flour
1 teaspoon ground cloves
1 teaspoon nutmeg
3 teaspoons cinnamon
1 teaspoon salt
1 pound pecans, chopped
1 pound raisins
1 teaspoon soda, dissolved in ⅛ cup boiling water

Cream butter and sugar. Add egg yolks and beat. Whip egg whites and fold in. Mix in vanilla. Remove ¼ cup flour and set aside. Sift flour with spices and salt. Mix ¼ cup flour with nuts and raisins. Add flour mixture to sugar mixture. Stir well. Add soda in water and mix. Add floured nuts and raisins. Mix well. Drop by spoonfuls about size of walnuts on cookie sheet. Bake at 375° for about 10 minutes.

Store in a sealed container.

AUNT ALICE'S SUGAR COOKIES

1 cup margarine
¾ cup sugar
2 eggs
1 teaspoon vanilla
1 teaspoon almond extract
2¾ cups flour
½ teaspoon salt
1 teaspoon baking powder

Cream margarine and sugar until light and fluffy. Add eggs, one at a time, beating well after each. Stir in vanilla and almond extract and mix well. Combine flour, salt and baking powder; add to creamed mixture. Mix well to blend. Dough will be stiff. Chill slightly; roll out on lightly floured board, cut into shapes. Bake on a greased baking sheet at 350° for 8 to 10 minutes or until light brown around the edges.

BUTTER SPRITZ COOKIES

1 cup butter
½ cup sugar
1 egg
½ teaspoon almond extract
  or 1 teaspoon vanilla
2¼ cups flour
½ teaspoon salt
¼ teaspoon baking powder

Cream butter and sugar, beat until fluffy. Beat in egg and flavoring. Mix together dry ingredients and blend into creamed mixture. Mix well. Color as desired. Put dough in cookie press and press out onto ungreased cookie sheet. Bake at 350° for 8 to 10 minutes or until lightly golden around the edges.

EASY OIL SUGAR COOKIES

2 eggs
⅔ cup vegetable oil
2 teaspoons vanilla
¾ cup sugar
2 cups flour
2 teaspoons baking powder
½ teaspoon salt

Beat eggs with fork and mix in remaining ingredients. Drop by spoon on ungreased cookie sheet. Stamp each cookie with a glass that has oil on bottom of it and dipped in sugar each time. Bake at 400° until slightly golden around the edges.

CREAM CHEESE SUGAR COOKIES

1 cup sugar
½ teaspoon salt
1 cup butter, softened
3 ounce package cream
   cheese
½ teaspoon almond extract
½ teaspoon vanilla
1 egg yolk (Reserve white)
2¾ cups flour

Combine all ingredients except flour; blend well. Stir in flour. Chill. Roll out on a lightly floured surface. Cut into desired shapes. Place on an ungreased cookie sheet. If desired brush with slightly beaten egg white then sprinkle with colored sugar. Bake at 375° for 7 to 10 minutes or until golden brown.

These are best after stored for a few days.

MAMA KNIGHT'S TEA CAKES

1 cup shortening
2 cups sugar
2 eggs
2 teaspoons baking powder
½ teaspoon soda
1 teaspoon lemon extract
5 cups flour
1 teaspoon nutmeg
¾ cup milk

Cream sugar and shortening. Add eggs and extract. Mix well. Add dry ingredients, which have been sifted together, alternately with milk. Roll out and cut with cookie cutter or drop by spoon on lightly greased cookie sheet. Bake at 350° until slightly browned around the edges.

NUT BUTTER BALLS OR POWDERED SUGAR CHRISTMAS COOKIES

1 cup soft butter or
   margarine
½ cup sugar
½ teaspoon salt
1 teaspoon almond extract
   or 2 teaspoons vanilla
2 cups flour
1 cup chopped pecans
Powdered sugar

Mix together all ingredients. Roll into balls. Bake on ungreased cookie sheet until light and brown at 325°. Allow to cool slightly but while still warm roll in the powdered sugar.

SPICE SUGAR COOKIES

1 pound margarine
1½ cups brown sugar, packed
1½ cups white sugar
3 eggs
⅓ cup water
1 teaspoon vanilla
5 cups flour, approximately
½ teaspoon soda
1 teaspoon cinnamon
1 cup chopped pecans

Cream margarine and sugars. Beat in eggs, one at a time. Mix in vanilla and water. Mix together flour, soda and cinnamon. Blend thoroughly into creamed mixture, about 1 cup at a time. Stir in pecans. Roll into roll in wax paper. Refrigerate overnight. Slice and bake on greased cookie sheet at 375° for 10 minutes.

GRANDMA'S TEA CAKES
(From her 1916 College Domestic Science Course)

1½ cups sugar
½ cup shortening
1 egg
2 teaspoons baking powder
Pinch of salt
1 teaspoon soda
1 cup sour milk
Flour-enough to make a dough like biscuits
Flavoring (I use vanilla and nutmeg)

Cream sugar and shortening; mix till light and fluffy. Add egg and beat well. Mix baking powder, salt, soda in 1 cup flour and add to creamed mixture. Add Flavoring. Mix in milk alternately with flour until it becomes a dough like biscuits. Roll out about ½ inch thick, cut with biscuit cutter. Bake on a lightly greased cookie sheet at 350° until very slightly golden around the edges.

OLD-FASHIONED TEA CAKES (100 Yr. Old Recipe)

4 cups flour
3 teaspoons baking powder
½ teaspoon salt
1 cup butter
2½ cups sugar
4 eggs
1 teaspoon vanilla
1 teaspoon almond extract

Sift together flour, baking powder and salt. Cream butter and sugar. Add eggs, one at a time, beating well after each. Add dry ingredients. Stir in flavorings. Roll out on well-floured board. Cut with cookie cutter. Bake on lightly greased cookie sheet at 325° until edges are very lightly browned.

MOTHER'S TEA CAKES OR SNICKERDOODLES

1 cup shortening
1 cup sugar
2 eggs
3 cups flour
2 teaspoons cream of tartar
1 teaspoon soda
½ teaspoon salt
1 teaspoon vanilla

Cream shortening and sugar until light and fluffy. Beat in eggs until creamy. Combine dry ingredients then add to shortening mixture until smooth. The dough will be stiff. Roll into balls the size of a thumb tip. Roll them in ¼ cup sugar and ½ teaspoon cinnamon mixed together. Place on greased baking sheet. Bake at 400° 5 to 6 minutes or until cookies flatten and crinkle on top.

GREAT SUGAR COOKIES

3 cups flour
1½ teaspoons baking
  powder
½ teaspoon salt
1 cup sugar
1 cup soft butter
1 egg, slightly beaten
3 tablespoons cream
1 teaspoon vanilla

Sift together flour, baking powder, salt and sugar. Cut in butter until particles are firm. Add egg, cream and vanilla. Blend thoroughly. Chill for several hours. Roll out to ⅛ inch, cut with cookie cutter. Bake on ungreased cookie sheet at 400° for 5 to 8 minutes or until delicately brown.

WHATA SUGAR COOKIE

1 cup sugar
1 cup powdered sugar
1 cup butter or margarine
2 eggs
1 cup oil
2 teaspoons vanilla
5 cups flour
1 teaspoon cream of tartar
¼ teaspoon salt
1 teaspoon soda

Cream sugars and butter; add eggs. Blend in oil and vanilla. Add the combined dry ingredients and mix well. Roll small amounts of dough into balls and place on ungreased cookie sheet. Flatten with a glass with a small amount of oil on the bottom then dipped into sugar. Bake at 350° for 10 minutes or until edges are slightly golden and center slightly firm.

GRANDMA'S 1916 SYRUP COOKIES

½ cup butter
½ cup maple syrup
1½ cups flour
½ teaspoon vanilla
2 teaspoons baking powder

Cream butter, add syrup slowly, beating to keep smooth. Add flour and baking powder. Add vanilla. Drop from spoon on a slightly greased cookie sheet. Flatten slightly. Bake at 350° for about 7 to 10 minutes.

TEXAS GOLD BARS

Crust:
1 package yellow cake mix
1 egg
1 stick margarine, melted

Filling:
8 ounces cream cheese
2 eggs
1 teaspoon vanilla
1 pound box powdered
  sugar

Topping:
Coconut
Pecans

Combine crust ingredients and mix well. Pat into a 9x13-inch pan. Beat together the filling ingredients. Pour over the crust. Sprinkle coconut and pecans on the top of cream cheese mixture. Bake at 325° for about 50 minutes. Cool and cut into squares.

from Grandma's
Candy Bowl

GRANDMA'S DATE LOAF CANDY

2¼ cups sugar
1 cup milk
1 cup (8 ounce) chopped
  dates
1 tablespoon margarine
1 teaspoon vanilla
1½ cups chopped pecans

Cook sugar, milk and dates over medium heat until soft ball stage (236°). Remove from heat, cool slightly and add margarine and vanilla. Cream until very stiff. Add pecans. Stir until mixture forms a large ball. Turn out onto wet cloth. Work with hands and cloth to form a slender loaf. Refrigerate until firm and slice.

DIVINITY

2½ cups sugar
½ cup light corn syrup
½ cup water
¼ teaspoon salt
2 egg whites
1 teaspoon vanilla
1 cup chopped pecans
  (optional)

Mix first 4 ingredients in a 2 quart saucepan. Cook over medium heat, stirring constantly, until mixture comes to boil. Reduce heat, cook, without stirring, until temperature reaches 265° or until small amount of syrup forms a ball in cold water that holds its shape, yet pliable. Just before temperature reaches 265° beat egg whites in a large bowl until stiff peaks form when beater is raised. Beating constantly on high speed of electric mixer, slowly pour hot syrup over egg whites. Continue beating until small amount holds soft peak when dropped from spoon. Mix in vanilla and nuts. Drop by teaspoonful onto waxed paper.

It is best not to make this candy on damp or rainy days.

Candy

CHOCO-NUT DIVINITY

3 cups sugar
½ cup water
⅓ cup white corn syrup
2 egg whites
½ cup walnuts, chopped
1 teaspoon vanilla
5 (1 ounce) squares
  semi-sweet chocolate cut
  into small pieces

Combine sugar, water and syrup in a 3 quart saucepan. Cook over medium heat, without stirring, to 250° on candy thermometer or until small amount of mixture forms a hard ball in cold water. Beat egg whites until stiff while mixture is cooking. When both are ready pour syrup in a fine stream over egg whites. Beat until mixture begins to stiffen. Stir in nuts, vanilla and chocolate pieces just until pieces are evenly distributed. (The chocolate pieces will give a chocolate marbled effect to the candy.) Drop by spoonfuls onto wax paper. Allow candy to cool completely. Makes about 72 pieces of candy.

EASY DIVINITY

2 cups sugar
Pinch of salt
½ cup water
1 jar (7 ounce)
  marshmellow creme
½ cup pecans, chopped

Bring sugar, salt and water to a boil. Boil for 2 minutes. Pour in marshmellow creme and stir until mixture is dull. Add nuts. Drop by spoonfuls on wax paper.

BROWN SUGAR FUDGE

2 cups brown sugar
1 cup milk
¼ teaspoon salt
2 squares unsweetened
  chocolate
2 tablespoons light corn
  syrup
2 tablespoons margarine
1 teaspoon vanilla
½ to 1 cup chopped nuts

Combine in saucepan brown sugar, milk, salt, chocolate and syrup. Cook, stirring constantly, over low heat until sugar is dissolved. Then cook, stirring occasionally, to 238° or until small amount of syrup forms a soft ball when dropped in cold water. Remove from heat, drop in but do not stir margarine. Cool to lukewarm (110°). Add vanilla; beat vigorously until it begins to harden. Stir in nuts; spread in greased pan. Cool, cut into squares.

CHOCOLATE SILK FUDGE

1 box powdered sugar
2 tablespoons margarine
½ teaspoon salt
⅔ cup evaporated milk,
  undiluted
1½ cups semi-sweet
  chocolate chips
2¼ cups minature
  marshmellows
½ cup chopped nuts
1 teaspoon vanilla

In a 2 quart saucepan combine powdered sugar, margarine, salt and milk; bring to boil over medium heat. Boil five minutes, stirring constantly. Remove from heat. Add chocolate chips, marshmellows, nuts and vanilla to cooked mixture. (DO NOT pour hot syrup over chocolate and marshmellows.) Beat vigorously until marshmellows and chocolate melt. Pour into well buttered 8x8x2-inch pan. Cool, then cut into squares.

CREAMY CHOCOLATE FUDGE

1 jar marshmellow creme
1½ cups sugar
⅔ cup evaporated milk
¼ cup butter or margarine
¼ teaspoon salt
11½ ounce package milk
   chocolate chips
6 ounce package
   semi-sweet chocolate
   chips
½ cup nuts
1 teaspoon vanilla

In a large saucepan, combine marshmellow creme, sugar, milk, butter and salt, bring to a full boil over moderate heat, stirring constantly. Boil for 5 minutes stirring constantly. Remove from heat, add chocolate chips, stir until chips melt and mixture is well blended. Stir in nuts and vanilla. Pour in buttered 8-inch square pan. Chill in refrigerator until firm, about 2 hours.

CREAMY COCOA FUDGE

½ cup margarine or butter
¾ cup cocoa
2 cups sugar
⅛ teaspoon salt
¾ cup evaporated milk
1 jar (7 ounce)
   marshmellow creme
1 teaspoon vanilla
1 cup pecans, chopped

Melt margarine in a 4 quart saucepan. Add cocoa and stir until smooth. Add sugar, salt, milk and marshmellow creme. Bring mixture to a full boil; boil, stirring constantly, for 5 minutes or until it reaches 226° on candy thermometer. Remove from heat and stir in vanilla. Cool 20 minutes. Beat with wooden spoon until mixture loses its gloss. Stir in nuts. Spread into 9x9x2-inch buttered pan. Cool, then cut into squares.

OLD-FASHIONED COCOA FUDGE

4 cups sugar
¾ cup water
¾ cup milk
⅓ to ½ cup cocoa
4 tablespoons margarine or
butter
⅛ teaspoon salt
1 teaspoon vanilla
1½ cups nuts

Combine sugar, water, milk, cocoa and margarine, boil without stirring until soft ball stage (236°). Remove from heat and let stand undisturbed until lukewarm (110°). Add salt, vanilla and nuts. Beat well until it begins to lose its gloss. Turn quickly into a buttered 9-inch square pan. Cool completely. Cut into squares.

MAPLE FUDGE

1 cup sugar
1 cup maple syrup
Pinch of salt
½ cup light cream
¾ cup walnuts, chopped

In a heavy saucepan stir together the sugar, syrup, salt and cream. Cook over a low heat. Bring to a boil, stirring constantly then boil without stirring until soft ball stage or 236° on candy thermometer. Remove from heat. Cool to lukewarm or 110° without stirring. Beat mixture until it loses it's gloss - usually for 12 to 15 minutes. The last few minutes of stirring stir in walnuts. Very quickly turn into a lightly buttered 8-inch square pan. When completely cool cut into squares.

MARSHMELLOW FUDGE

2¾ cups miniature
  marshmellows
½ cup evaporated milk
2 tablespoons butter
¾ cup sugar
⅛ teaspoon salt
6 ounce package chocolate
  chips
½ teaspoon vanilla
¼ cup chopped nuts

Combine 2 cups marshmellows, milk, butter, sugar and salt in a heavy saucepan. Stirring, bring to a full boil over high heat. Reduce heat to medium, stirring constantly boil 3 minutes. Remove from heat; add chips and vanilla. Beat until chips melt; stir in nuts. Arrange remaining marshmellows in buttered 8x8x4-inch pan; pour chocolate mixture over marshmellows. Chill until firm.

AFTER DINNER MINTS

White of 1 egg, not beaten
1 teaspoon water
1 box powdered sugar
Few drops of peppermint
  extract

Mix all ingredients together. You can add a drop or two of food coloring to make pastel mints. Roll small amounts of mixture into balls and place on wax paper then flatten with a fork. Allow to harden slightly.

PEANUT BRITTLE FROM A PEANUT GROWER

3 cups sugar
1 cup white corn syrup
½ cup water
3 cups raw peanuts
1 teaspoon salt
2 teaspoons soda, heaping
3 teaspoon butter

Boil sugar, syrup and water until thread spins (232°). Add peanuts and stir constantly after peanuts are added. Cook until it turns a brownish gold. Remove from fire; add butter, salt and soda (it foams up at this point). You have to work fast. Pour onto 2 buttered cookie sheets and tilt to spread over pans. Cool completely then break into pieces.

RED PEANUT PATTIES

3 cups sugar
1 cup water
1 cup light corn syrup
1 pound (3½ cups) raw
  Spanish peanuts
6 drops red food coloring
¼ cup margarine
Pinch of salt

Combine sugar, water and corn syrup in a saucepan. Bring to a boil then add peanuts and coloring. Cook until hard ball stage (250°). Remove from heat and add margarine and salt. Beat until it thickens. Pour into greased muffin pans just enough to make a ½ inch thick patty. Allow to cool completely. Makes about 24 patties.

BOB'S MOTHER'S PEANUT BUTTER ROLL

4 cups white sugar
½ cup white corn syrup
½ cup warm water
3 egg whites
Peanut Butter

In a saucepan stir together sugar, syrup and water. Let boil until hard ball forms when dropped in cold water. Beat the egg whites until stiff. Pour the sugar syrup into the egg whites in a slow stream while mixer is beating. Beat until stiff enough to spread; then spread on a piece of buttered wax paper. Spread with peanut butter and roll up like a jelly roll when cool enough to handle. Wrap in wax paper; cool then cut into slices.

GRANDMA'S PENUCHE

2⅔ cups light brown sugar
¾ cup milk
3 tablespoons butter or
  margarine
1 teaspoon vanilla
2 cups chopped nuts
  (optional)

Boil sugar, milk and butter, stirring as little as possible until it forms a soft ball in cold water (236°). Remove from heat. Set in a pan of cold water. When cool, add vanilla and nuts. Beat until creamy. Pour into buttered pan. Let set until firm then cut into squares.

BUTTERMILK PRALINES

3 cups sugar
1 cup buttermilk
1 teaspoon soda
½ pound butter
2 tablespoons light corn
  syrup
⅛ teaspoon salt
4 cups pecans, broken

Combine all ingredients except pecans in a saucepan. Cook over high heat, stirring often. Cook to 250° on candy thermometer. Remove from heat. Stir in pecans. Stir a few minutes until not so glossy. Spoon onto wax paper. Makes about 60 pralines.

CREOLE PRALINES

3 cups sugar
1 cup water
1 teaspoon vinegar
1 tablespoon margarine
3 cups chopped pecans

Combine sugar, water and vinegar. Cook to soft ball stage (236°). Add margarine and nuts. Remove from heat. Beat until mixture begins to thicken. Drop by teaspoon onto wax paper. Allow to cool.

OLDTIME PRALINES

3 cups sugar
1 cup cream or rich milk
1 teaspoon grated orange rind
1 cup sugar (for browning)
1 teaspoon vanilla
2 cups pecans
Dash of salt

Boil 3 cups sugar with cream and rind in a large saucepan until it forms a soft ball when dropped into cold water. While this is cooking melt the 1 cup of sugar in a heavy frying pan, stirring constantly until it is pale golden brown. When both are ready add carmelized sugar to first mixture. (Using a long spoon to stir - it foams up.) Test immediately for soft ball stage (236°), if it is, remove from heat and let cool to almost lukewarm (110°). Add vanilla, nuts and salt; beat until stiff and creamy. Drop in large clumps on a buttered cookie sheet. Cool completely.

PECAN PRALINES

2 cups brown sugar, packed
¼ cup water
2½ cups pecans
1 tablespoon margarine or butter
½ teaspoon vanilla

Combine sugar and water in a saucepan. Bring to a boil, stirring constantly. Stir in pecans. Cook until soft ball stage (235°). Remove from heat; stir in margarine. Immediately drop by spoonfuls onto wax paper. Cool completely.

WESTERN PRALINES

2 cups dark brown sugar,
  packed or white sugar
1 teaspoon soda
1 cup buttermilk
⅛ teaspoon salt
2 tablespoons margarine or
  butter
2 cups pecan halves,
  unbroken

In a 4 quart saucepan combine sugar, soda, buttermilk and salt. Cook over medium heat, stirring constantly for 5 minutes or until candy thermometer reaches 210°. Add margarine and 1 cup of pecans. Continue cooking, stirring constantly, to 230° or until a very soft ball is formed when dropped in cold water. Remove from heat; cool about 7 to 10 minutes. Beat until mixture becomes thick and creamy. Working quickly, drop by spoonfuls onto wax paper or buttered foil. Press remaining cup of pecans into candy. Makes about 30 pralines.

GRANDMA'S SOUR CREAM CANDY
From the early 1900's

2 cups sugar
1 cup sour cream
Dash of salt
1 tablespoon vanilla
2 tablespoons butter
½ to 1 cup chopped pecans

Combine sugar, sour cream and salt in a saucepan and cook over a medium high heat. Stir occasionally. Cool to soft ball stage (238°). Remove from heat. Add vanilla, butter and pecans. Beat until thick. Pour into a buttered dish. Cut into squares when slightly cooled.

SUGAR PLUMS

2 boxes or 1 bag (2 pound)
  powdered sugar
1 stick margarine
1 can sweetened condensed
  milk
1 can (7 ounce) coconut
1 to 2 cups chopped nuts
1 small jar maraschino
  cherries, cut up
3 (6 ounce) packages
  chocolate chips
¾ bar paraffin

Mix all ingredients, except chocolate chips and paraffin, together in a large bowl. Mix until well blended. Roll into small balls. Put in the refrigerator on a tray with wax paper, chill. Put chocolate chips and paraffin in top of double boiler and melt. Insert toothpick into candy and dip one at a time into chocolate. Place back on wax paper to cool.

TOFFEE

1½ cups margarine
1¾ cups sugar
⅓ cup corn syrup, light or
  dark
2 cups chopped nuts
4 (1 ounce) squares
  semi-sweet chocolate,
  melted

Melt margarine in 2 quart saucepan; add sugar and cook until dissolved. Add syrup and cook over low heat until mixture reaches 290°. Stir in 1½ cups nuts. Pour into ungreased 9x13-inch baking sheet. Cool. Spread melted chocolate over toffee; sprinkle with ½ cup nuts. Allow to cool completely then break into pieces.

from Grandma's
Pie Tin

SHORTENING PASTRY

1 cup flour
½ teaspoon salt
⅓ cup shortening
2 to 3 tablespoon ice water

Combine dry ingredients. Work in shortening with a fork until well combined. Sprinkle with ice water and work with a fork until all particles are moistened and is workable. Roll out on a floured surface.

Double recipe for a pie needing a top crust.

OIL PASTRY

2 cups flour
1½ teaspoons salt
1 tablespoon sugar
½ cup oil
¼ cup milk

Combine dry ingredients. Pour in oil and milk. Stir with fork until well combined. Roll out between 2 pieces of wax paper.

NEVER-FAIL PIE CRUST

3 cups flour
1 teaspoon baking powder
1 teaspoon salt
1⅓ cups shortening
1 egg
5 to 6 tablespoons cold
   water
1 tablespoon vinegar

Blend dry ingredients with shortening. Add egg and liquids. Form into roll, wrap in wax paper. Store in refrigerator. When ready to use, take off as much as needed, allow to warm to room temperature. Roll out on floured surface. Makes 3 single pie crusts.

COBBLER DOUGH

3 cups flour
5 teaspoons baking powder
1½ teaspoons salt
3 tablespoons sugar
1 teaspoon cream of tartar
¾ cup margarine, melted
1 cup milk
1 egg, beaten

In mixing bowl combine all dry ingredients. Mix in melted margarine, milk and beaten egg, mix thoroughly. Roll out on floured surface about ⅓ inch thick. Place in a 12-inch square baking dish or a 9x13-inch baking pan. Add prepared fruit. Cut remaining dough into strips and lay across fruit to make a lattice top. Sprinkle top with cinnamon and sugar. Bake at 350° for 40 to 50 minutes.

MERINGUE

3 egg whites
6 tablespoons sugar
¼ teaspoon cream of tartar

Beat egg whites until frothy. Gradually add sugar and cream of tartar. Beat until soft peaks form.

Pile on top of pie making sure that meringue seals to the crust all around the pie.

Brown at 350° for 8 to 10 minutes or until meringue is golden.

EASY AND DELICIOUS FRUIT COBBLER

1 cup flour
2 teaspoons baking powder
⅛ teaspoon salt
1 cup sugar
1 cup milk
½ cup margarine
1 teaspoon vanilla
2 cups fresh peaches or
   any fruit desired

Mix together flour, baking powder, salt and sugar. Add milk and mix well. Melt margarine in a 9x9-inch pan. Pour batter into center of melted margarine, but do not stir. Pour prepared peaches over batter. Bake at 350° for 50 minutes.

To Prepare Peaches:
Slice fresh peaches in a bowl. Sprinkle with 1 cup sugar or less depending on taste, 1 heaping tablespoon flour and a dash of salt. Toss together. Let set while making batter so it can make a syrup.

APPLE COBBLER

5 cups peeled, sliced
   apples
¾ cup sugar
2 tablespoons flour
½ teaspoon cinnamon
¼ teaspoon salt
¼ cup water
1 teaspoon vanilla
1 tablespoon margarine,
   softened

Combine all ingredients except margarine and mix gently. Spoon into a lightly greased 9-inch square pan; dot with margarine. Set aside while preparing topping. Spoon topping over apples in 9 equal portions. Batter will spread while baking. Bake at 375° for 35 to 40 minutes.

Topping:
½ cup flour
½ cup sugar
½ teaspoon baking powder
¼ teaspoon salt
2 tablespoons margarine,
   softened
1 egg, slightly beaten

Topping:
Combine all ingredients and mix well with a fork.

GRANDMA'S APPLE PIE

Line a pie pan with pastry. Slice into it thin slices of tart apples, enough to fill. For each apple use 2 tablespoons sugar and sprinkle over apples. Sprinkle apples with cinnamon to taste. Sprinkle 2 or 3 tablespoons of warm water. Put a top crust on pie. Dot top with butter. Sprinkle with sugar and cinnamon. Bake at 375° until crust is golden brown.

TEXAS RICH APPLE PIE

6 to 8 sliced tart apples
½ cup brown sugar
3 tablespoons flour
Pinch of salt
1 teaspoon cinnamon
1 tablespoon lemon juice
½ teaspoon nutmeg
Crumb Topping, recipe
  follows

Combine dry ingredients and pour over apple slices in a bowl. Add lemon juice. Toss until slices are well coated. Turn into a 9 inch pie shell, heaping in center. Top with Crumb Topping. Bake at 450° for 10 minutes, then reduce to 350° and bake 40-50 minutes more.

Crumb Topping:
⅓ cup brown sugar
⅓ cup flour
1 teaspoon cinnamon
¼ cup margarine, softened

Crumb Topping:
Mix together well with a fork until all is combined to make crumbs.

APPLE CRISP

3 cups apples, sliced
¼ cup hot water
1 cup oatmeal
¼ cup margarine
½ cup brown sugar
¼ cup flour
Dash of salt
Cinnamon to taste

Place apples in baking dish and add hot water. Mix all ingredients together well and sprinkle over the apples. Bake at 350° for 1 hour.

BANANA CREAM PIE

1½ cups sugar
½ cup flour
⅛ teaspoon salt
2 eggs
2 cups milk
1 tablespoon margarine
1 teaspoon vanilla
3 medium bananas
Whipped Cream,
   sweetened

In medium saucepan mix sugar, flour, salt and eggs with a portable mixer. Gradually add milk and beat until smooth. Cook over medium heat, stirring constantly, until it thickens. Remove from heat. Add margarine and vanilla and blend well. Refrigerate. When cool mash one banana and stir into pudding mixture. Slice other 2 bananas and put on bottom of baked 9 inch pie crust. Spoon pudding on top of bananas. Spread sweetened whipped cream over top and refrigerate.

BLACKBERRY COBBLER

4 to 6 cups ripe
   blackberries
1¼ cups sugar
2 tablespoons flour
¼ cup water or
2 tablespoons water and
2 tablespoons blackberry
   brandy or wine

In a saucepan cook berries with 1 cup sugar and water until berries are soft. Mix flour and ¼ cup sugar and add to berries. Cook stirring constantly until mixture is slightly thick. Spoon into pastry lined cobbler pan. Cover with pastry strips. Dot with butter. Bake at 425° until pastry is browned.

BLUEBERRY PIE

1 quart blueberries,
  washed and drained
½ cup water
1 cup sugar
2 tablespoons cornstarch
Pinch of salt
3 tablespoons water
Grated lemon rind

Cook berries over low heat with ½ cup water and sugar and lemon rind until berries are soft. Combine cornstarch and salt with 3 tablespoons of water, stir slowly into berry mixture. Cook for 5 minutes. Cool. Pour into unbaked pie shell and top with pastry. Bake at 450° for 10 minutes, then reduce heat to 375° for 30 minutes.

BROWN SUGAR PIE

3 cups brown sugar
2 tablespoons flour
3 eggs
1 cup milk
1 teaspoon vanilla

Beat eggs well, mix in remaining ingredients. Pour into an unbaked 9 inch pie shell. Bake at 325° for 35 to 40 minutes.

GRANDMA'S WW II BUTTERMILK PIE

3 eggs
1 cup sugar
3 tablespoons flour
½ cup margarine, melted
1 cup buttermilk
1 teaspoon lemon extract
1 teaspoon grated lemon
  rind
⅛ teaspoon nutmeg

Beat eggs slightly, add sugar and flour. Add melted margarine and mix well. Add buttermilk, lemon extract, rind and nutmeg. Mix together well and pour into a 9-inch unbaked pie shell. Bake at 325° until set.

(You can leave out the lemon extract and rind and add 1 teaspoon vanilla)

MOTHER'S BUTTERSCOTCH PIE

1½ cups brown sugar
3 tablespoons butter
4 tablespoons cream
1½ cups milk
6 tablespoons cornstarch
2 egg yolks
1 teaspoon vanilla

Cook brown sugar, butter and cream in a heavy pan until thick and brown. The browner the more butterscotch flavor. Combine milk with cornstarch and egg yolks. Mix well, then stir into sugar mixture, stir constantly. Cook until thick. Pour into a baked pie crust. Top with meringue and brown.

GRANDMA'S BUTTERSCOTCH CUSTARD PIE - 1920's

1½ cups brown sugar
½ cup butter
3 egg yolks
Pinch of salt
½ cup chopped nuts
1 tablespoon cornstarch

Cream butter and sugar, then add egg yolks. Add remaining ingredients. Bake in an unbaked pie shell at 350° until set.

GRANDMA'S CARMEL PIE

¾ cup sugar and ½ cup to brown
3 tablespoons flour
1½ cups sweet milk
3 egg yolks
2 tablespoons butter
1 teaspoon vanilla

In a pan melt and brown ½ cup sugar, add remaining sugar mixed with flour. Pour in milk and egg yolks. Cook and stir until smooth and thick. Add butter and vanilla. Cool. Pour into a baked pie crust and top with meringue and brown.

OLD-FASHIONED CHERRY PIE

1 cup sugar
¼ cup flour
¼ teaspoon salt
½ cup juice from cherries
3 cups canned tart red
  pitted cherries, drained
1 tablespoon margarine,
  softened
4 drops almond extract
7 to 10 drops red food
  coloring

Combine sugar, flour and salt; stir in juice. Cook over medium heat, stirring until thick; then cook 1 minute longer. Add cherries, butter, extract and coloring. Let set while pie shell is prepared. Fill a 9 inch pie shell with filling. Top with lattice crust. Bake at 450° for 10 minutes. Reduce heat to 350° for 45 minutes more.

AUNT LOUISE'S CHESS PIE

2 cups sugar
1 tablespoon corn meal
1 tablespoon flour
3 eggs
1 tablespoon vanilla
Pinch of salt
1 cup evaporated milk
2 tablespoons butter or
  margarine

Combine all ingredients and mix well. Pour into an unbaked pie shell. Bake at 350° for 10 minutes; reduce heat to 250° and bake for 45 minutes more.

LEMON CHESS PIE

2 cups sugar
1 heaping tablespoon flour
1 tablespoon cornmeal
4 eggs
⅓ cup lemon juice
1 stick margarine, melted

Mix all ingredients together. Pour into an unbaked pie shell. Bake at 375° until set and browned.

AUNT ALICE'S CHESS PIE

1 cup sugar
1 stick margarine
4 eggs
1 tablespoon cornmeal
1 tablespoon vinegar
1 teaspoon vanilla

Cream sugar and margarine. Add other ingredients. Pour into un-baked pie shell. Bake at 300° for 40 to 60 minutes or until set.

GRANDMA'S 1940's COCOA FLUFF PIE

¾ cup sugar
½ teaspoon salt
2 tablespoons cornstarch
2 tablespoons flour
½ cup cocoa
2 cups milk, lukewarm
1 egg yolk, slightly beaten
1 tablespoon margarine
1 teaspoon vanilla
Meringue - recipe below

Mix together in top of a double boiler pan the dry ingredients. Stir in milk. Bring to a boil over low heat and boil 3 minutes; stir-ring constantly. Remove from heat. Slowly stir a small amount of hot mixture into egg yolk. Then blend into pan of hot mixture. Place over boiling water and cook about 10 minutes, stirring occa-sionally. Remove from heat. Blend in margarine. Cool slightly. Stir in vanilla. Fold in meringue. Pour into 8 inch baked pie crust. Chill 2 to 3 hours before serving.

Meringue:
1 egg white
⅛ teaspoon cream of tartar
2 tablespoons sugar

Meringue:
Beat egg white until frothy, add cream of tartar. Continue beating until stiff enough to hold a point. Gradually beat in sugar, continue beating until mixture is stiff and glossy.

EASY CHOCOLATE PIE

½ cup milk
¼ cup margarine
1¼ cups sugar
¼ cup cocoa
1 tablespoon flour
Pinch of salt
1 teaspoon vanilla
2 eggs

Heat milk and margarine together until margarine is melted. Mix together sugar, cocoa, flour and salt. Add to milk and mix well. Stir in vanilla. Mix in slightly beaten eggs. Pour into an unbaked 9-inch pie shell. Bake at 350° for 50 to 60 minutes or until set. Cool. Serve topped with whipped cream or ice cream.

GRANDMA'S CHOCOLATE PIE

5 eggs (reserve whites of 4 for meringue)
5 tablespoons cocoa
5 tablespoons flour
1⅔ cups sugar
½ teaspoon salt
2⅔ cups milk
1 teaspoon vanilla
2 tablespoons margarine

Separate the eggs, leaving 1 whole egg with the yolks. Mix together the sugar, flour, cocoa and salt in a saucepan. Gradually stir in the milk. Add egg yolks and 1 whole egg to mixture and stir well. Cook long enough to be thick for a pie, stirring constantly so it will not stick on the bottom of pan. It is best to use a wisk so that it will not have lumps. Remove from heat and cool slightly. Add vanilla and margarine. Cool. Pour into a baked 10-inch pie crust or 2 (8-inch) pie crusts. Top with meringue and brown.

This takes a while to thicken and you have to stir for a while but it is certainly worth the effort.

CHOCOLATE FUDGE BROWNIE PIE

1 stick margarine, melted
¼ cup cocoa
2 eggs, beaten
1 cup sugar
¼ cup flour
½ teaspoon vanilla
1 cup chopped pecans
½ cup coconut (optional)

Blend cocoa into melted margarine. Add remaining ingredients, mix well. Pour into unbaked 9-inch pie shell. Bake at 350° for 25 minutes or until set. Cool and refrigerate. Serve topped with whipped cream or ice cream.

GRANDMOTHER'S CHOCOLATE PIE

3 squares unsweetened
  chocolate
¼ cup cornstarch
1 cup sugar
½ teaspoon salt
2½ cups milk
3 egg yolks
1 tablespoon margarine
2 teaspoons vanilla

Melt and cool chocolate. Combine cornstarch, sugar and salt. Stir in milk and chocolate. Cook over medium heat, stir constantly. Boil for 1 minute. Blend small amount of chocolate mixture with beaten egg yolks; then stir back into chocolate mixture. Cook 1 minute. Remove from heat. Stir in margarine and vanilla. Cool slightly. Pour into baked pie crust and top with meringue and brown.

Pies

MEMORY SEEKERS CHOCOLATE FUDGE PIE

½ cup margarine
3 squares (1 ounce each) unsweetened chocolate
4 eggs, slightly beaten
3 tablespoons white corn syrup
1½ cups sugar
¼ teaspoon salt
1 teaspoon vanilla

Melt margarine and chocolate in a double boiler and cool. Beat eggs; add remaining ingredients. Add cooled chocolate. Mix well. Pour into unbaked pie shell. Bake at 350° for 30 minutes or until top begins to crack.

The center is moist and fudgy.

CHOCOLATE SYRUP PIE

1 cup sugar
2 tablespoons flour
Dash of baking powder
3 eggs, separated
2 cups milk
1½ teaspoons vanilla
1 tablespoon butter, melted
½ cup chocolate syrup

Combine sugar, flour and baking powder. Add egg yolks beaten with milk, vanilla and butter. Add chocolate syrup. Pour into pie shell. Bake at 350° for 40 minutes or until set. Make meringue and put on top of baked pie. Brown in a hot oven.

GERMAN SWEET CHOCOLATE PIE

1 package (4 ounce) German Chocolate
¼ cup butter
1⅔ cups (14½ oz) can evaporated milk
1½ cups sugar
3 tablespoons cornstarch
⅛ teaspoon salt
2 eggs
1 teaspoon vanilla
1⅓ cups coconut
½ cup chopped pecans

Melt chocolate with butter over low heat, stirring until blended. Remove from heat; gradually blend in milk. Mix sugar, cornstarch and salt thoroughly. Beat in eggs and vanilla. Gradually blend in chocolate milk mixture. Pour into unbaked 10-inch pie shell. Combine coconut and nuts; sprinkle over filling. Bake at 375° for 45 minutes. Filling will be soft but will set while cooling. Cool at least 4 hours before cutting.

COCONUT CUSTARD PIE

1 cup milk
1 cup coconut
¼ cup margarine
1 cup sugar
1 tablespoon flour
3 eggs
1 teaspoon vanilla

Pour milk over coconut and set aside. Cream margarine, sugar and flour. Add eggs and beat well. Add milk and coconut and flavoring. Pour into unbaked pie shell. Bake at 350° for 30 to 40 minutes or until golden brown and firm.

GRANDMA'S COCONUT CREAM PIE

½ cup sugar
½ cup flour
¼ teaspoon salt
3 cups milk
3 egg yolks, slightly beaten
1 cup flaked coconut
3 tablespoons butter
1½ teaspoons vanilla

Meringue:
3 egg whites
6 tablespoons sugar
¼ teaspoon cream of tartar

Mix sugar, flour and salt in a saucepan. Add milk gradually; stirring constantly. Cook until mixture boils. Mix small portion of hot mixture with egg yolks and return to saucepan. Boil for 2 minutes; stirring constantly. Remove from heat. Add coconut, butter and vanilla. Cool. Pour into cooled pie shell. Top with meringue and sprinkle ¼ cup coconut on top. Brown at 350°.

GRANDMOTHER'S CRACKER PIE

4 egg whites
1 cup sugar
½ teaspoon salt
1 teaspoon vanilla
1 teaspoon baking powder
1 cup graham cracker
  crumbs or Ritz cracker
  crumbs
1 cup chopped pecans

Beat egg whites to almost stiff. Add sugar gradually. Fold in remaining ingredients. Bake in a 9-inch greased pie pan at 350° for 25 to 30 minutes. Cool.

CRANBERRY PIE

2 cups sugar
½ teaspoon cinnamon
1 tablespoon flour
¼ teaspoon salt
½ cup water
4 cups fresh cranberries
1 tablespoon orange rind
2 tablespoons margarine

Combine sugar, cinnamon, flour and salt; add water and mix well. Add cranberries and cook slowly until the skins pop; stir occasionally. Add orange rind and margarine. Pour into an unbaked pie shell and top with strips of pastry. Seal edges. Bake at 400° for 40 to 50 minutes.

JEFF DAVIS PIE

2 cups sugar
1 cup butter or margarine
1 tablespoon flour
¼ teaspoon salt
1 teaspoon vanilla
6 eggs, beaten lightly
1 cup milk

Cream sugar and butter. Blend flour, salt and vanilla into mixture and beat well. Add eggs then stir in milk. Pour filling into 2 (9-inch) unbaked pie shells. Bake at 450° for 10 minutes, then reduce heat to 350° for 30 minutes more or until filling is firm.

VANILLA CUSTARD PIE

4 slightly beaten eggs
½ cup sugar
¼ teaspoon salt
½ teaspoon vanilla
2½ cups milk, scalded
Nutmeg

Blend eggs with sugar, salt and vanilla. Gradually stir in scalded milk. Pour into unbaked pie shell. Sprinkle top with nutmeg. Bake at 350° for 35 to 40 minutes or until knife inserted 1 inch from edge comes out clean. Cool on rack. Cool before serving.

(To prevent spilling the liquid filling, pour it into the pie shell after it is placed on the oven rack.)

FRUIT SALAD PIE

1 cup chilled whipping
cream
2 tablespoon sugar
1 teaspoon vanilla
½ cup miniature
marshmallows
1 tablespoon finely
chopped pecans
4 cups mixed fruit: green
and red grapes,
strawberries, peaches,
plums, apples, bananas,
mandrine oranges,
cherries

Beat whipping cream, sugar and
vanilla in a chilled bowl until
stiff. Fold in fruit and marshmallows. Spoon into a graham
crackers pie shell. Sprinkle with
nuts. Cover and refrigerate for at
least 1 hour.

*(An 8 ounce container of frozen
whipped topping, thawed, can be
used in place of whipping cream,
sugar and vanilla.)*

WORLD WAR I KARO PIE

2 eggs, beaten
¾ cup sugar
1 cup dark Karo syrup
1 tablespoon corn meal
1 teaspoon vanilla
1 teaspoon lemon extract
¼ cup butter, melted

Mix all ingredients together. Pour
into a 9-inch unbaked pie shell.
Bake at 325° for 45 minutes or
until set.

GRANDMA'S OLD-FASHIONED LEMON CAKE PIE

2 eggs, separated
1 cup milk
1 cup sugar
¼ cup flour
⅓ cup lemon juice
1 teaspoon lemon rind

Beat egg yolks; then beat in milk.
Mix together sugar and flour; add
to milk and eggs. Add lemon juice
and rind. Fold in egg whites that
have been beaten stiff but not dry.
Pour into unbaked pie shell. Bake
at 425° for 25 minutes or until
set. Cool before serving.

QUEEN OF LEMON MERINGUE PIES

½ cup cornstarch
1½ cups sugar
¼ teaspoon salt
1¾ cups water
4 egg yolks, slightly beaten
2 tablespoons margarine
1 tablespoon grated lemon
  peel
½ cup lemon juice
½ teaspoon lemon extract
1 teaspoon vinegar

Blend cornstarch, sugar and salt in a medium saucepan. Stir in water gradually. Cook over medium heat, stirring constantly, until mixture comes to a boil. Boil 1 minute. Stir about ½ cup of mixture into egg yolks then pour back into the pan. Cook over low heat, stirring constantly, for 2 minutes. Remove from heat. Add margarine, lemon peel, lemon juice, lemon extract and vinegar. Cool slightly. Pour into baked pie crust, cover with merinque and brown slightly.

GRANDMA'S LEMON PIE - 1920's

3 egg yolks
1 cup sugar
2 tablespoons flour
1 cup water
⅛ teaspoon salt
1 large lemon - use juice,
  some of pulp and rind
1 tablespoon butter

In a saucepan stir egg yolks, sugar and flour. Place on medium high heat and stir in water, salt and lemon juice, pulp and rind. Stir constantly until bubbles form. Continue to stir vigorously about 2 minutes until it is thick. Remove from heat and stir in butter. Pour into a glass bowl and refrigerate. When completely cool pour into baked pie crust. Top with meringue and brown.

GRANDMOTHER'S LEMON MERINGUE PIE

1 cup sugar
¼ teaspoon salt
¼ cup flour
3 tablespoons cornstarch
2 cups water
3 egg yolks
2 tablespoons margarine
⅓ cup lemon juice
2 teaspoons grated lemon
    rind

Combine sugar, salt, flour and cornstarch with ½ cup water. Heat remaining water and add sugar mixture. Cook over low heat until thickened and clear; about 20 minutes. Beat egg yolks, add a small amount of hot mixture to them and return to first mixture, stirring constantly. When thick remove from heat, about 5 minutes. Stir in butter, lemon juice and rind. Pour into baked pie crust and cool. Top with meringue and brown. Cool.

OLD-FASHIONED MOLASSES PIE

1¼ cups molasses
1 tablespoon margarine
3 eggs
2 tablespoons flour
¾ cup sugar

Place molasses and margarine in a saucepan and let come to a boil. Beat eggs until light and fluffy. Mix flour and sugar then add to eggs; add this mixture to molasses. Pour into unbaked pie shell. Bake at 325° for 30 minutes or until set.

OATMEAL PIE

¾ cup sugar
¾ cup dark corn syrup
¾ cup quick cooking
    oatmeal
½ cup margarine, melted
½ cup coconut
2 eggs, well beaten

Mix all ingredients together and pour into a pie shell. Bake at 350° for 50 to 60 minutes. Cool. Serve topped with whipped cream.

OSGOOD PIE

½ cup margarine or butter
2 cups sugar
4 egg yolks, beaten
1 cup raisins
1 cup pecans
½ teaspoon cinnamon
½ teaspoon cloves
4 egg whites

Cream butter and sugar until fluffy. Add beaten egg yolks, raisins, pecans and spices. Fold in stiffly beaten egg whites. Pour into an unbaked 9-inch pie shell. Bake at 325° for 50 minutes.

PEACH COBBLER

8 cups sliced fresh peaches
⅓ cup flour
2 cups sugar
1 teaspoon cinnamon
1 cup water
½ cup margarine, melted
1 teaspoon almond extract
Pastry, recipe follows

Mix flour into sugar, add cinnamon and water; mix well. Toss in peaches. Set aside. Roll out ¾ of pastry to ⅛ inch thick on a lightly floured surface. Fit pastry into a 13x9x2-inch baking dish. Spoon in peach mixture. Roll out remaining pastry to ¼ inch thick. Cut into strips and arrange over peaches. Bake at 350° for 1 hour.

Pastry:
3 cups flour
1½ teaspoons salt
¾ teaspoon baking powder
¾ cup shortening
6 to 8 tablespoons ice water

Pastry:
Combine dry ingredients; cut in shortening until mixture resembles coarse meal. Sprinkle ice water over surface, stir with a fork until dry ingredients are moistened.

PEANUT BUTTER PIE

1 baked pie crust
1 cup powdered sugar
½ cup peanut butter
1 box vanilla pudding,
  cooked or
Cream Filling, recipe
  follows
Whipped Cream or
  Meringue

Mix peanut butter and powdered sugar until crumbly. Put half of crumb mixture in baked pie crust. Fill with prepared pudding mix or cream filling that is cooled. Spread top with whipped cream or meringue. Sprinkle remainder of peanut butter crumbs on top. If meringue is used brown pie in the oven. Chill thoroughly.

Cream Filling:
4 tablespoons cornstarch
3 egg yolks
⅔ cup sugar
2 cups milk
¼ teaspoon salt
1 teaspoon vanilla

Cream Filling:
Combine all ingredients in a saucepan. Cook over medium heat until thick. Stir constantly.

Also good with chocolate pudding or chocolate filling.

TEXAS PECAN PIE

1½ cups dark brown sugar,
  packed
½ cup sugar
¼ cup water
2 tablespoons flour
½ teaspoon salt
2 eggs
½ cup evaporated milk
1½ cups pecan halves
¾ teaspoon vanilla

Combine first 5 ingredients in a small mixing bowl and mix well. Beat in eggs, one at a time. Add milk and mix well. Stir in pecans and vanilla. Pour into an unbaked 9-inch pie shell. Bake at 400° for 10 minutes, then reduce heat to 350° and bake 35 to 40 minutes more or until set.

GRANDMOTHER'S PECAN PIE

¾ cup sugar
2 tablespoons flour
1 teaspoon salt
1 cup dark corn syrup
2 eggs
½ cup canned evaporated
  milk
1 cup pecans
1 teaspoon vanilla

Mix together sugar, flour and salt. Stir in corn syrup. Beat in eggs, one at a time. Mix in milk, pecans and vanilla. Stir well to mix. Pour into unbaked pie shell. Bake at 375° for 50 minutes or until firm.

DALLAS PECAN PIE

1½ cups white sugar
1 tablespoon flour
1½ cups white syrup
3 eggs, well beaten
1 tablespoon butter
1 teaspoon vanilla
1½ cups coconut
2 cups pecans

Combine first 3 ingredients. Add melted butter. Add eggs and mix well. Add vanilla and mix in. Add coconut and pecans. Pour into unbaked pie shell and bake at 325° for 1 hour.

MAMMA'S PECAN PIE

3 eggs, slightly beaten
½ cup brown sugar
1 cup white corn syrup
½ teaspoon salt
1 teaspoon vanilla
¼ cup margarine, melted
1 cup pecans

Mix ingredients in the order given. Pour into an unbaked pie shell. Bake at 350° for 30 to 45 minutes or until set.

AUNT ALICE'S PECAN PIE

1 cup dark Karo syrup
1 teaspoon vanilla
3 eggs, slightly beaten
⅛ teaspoon salt
1 cup sugar
2 tablespoons margarine, melted
2 cups pecans, chopped

Mix together all ingredients; adding pecans last. Pour into un-baked pie shell. Bake at 400° for 15 minutes. Reduce heat to 350° and bake 30 to 35 minutes longer or until set.

CHOCOLATE CHIP PECAN PIE

3 eggs, slightly beaten
1¼ cups white corn syrup
⅛ teaspoon salt
1 teaspoon vanilla
½ cup sugar
1 cup pecan halves
1 cup chocolate chips
Whipping cream

Combine eggs, corn syrup, salt, vanilla and sugar; mix well. Stir in pecans and chocolate chips. Pour into unbaked 9-inch pie shell. Bake at 450° for 10 min-utes; then reduce heat to 350° and bake 45 to 50 minutes more or until knife inserted in center comes out clean. Cool. Serve topped with whipped cream.

AUNT MINNIE'S PECAN PIE

4 eggs
2 cups dark corn syrup
2 tablespoons melted butter
1 teaspoon vanilla
1½ cups pecans

With a wire whisk beat the eggs in a mixing bowl for about 30 sec-onds. Slowly pour in the syrup and continue to beat until they are well combined. Beat in melted butter and vanilla. Stir in pecans. Pour into unbaked pie shell. Bake at 350° for 35 to 40 minutes or until filling is firm.

MY BEST PECAN PIE

½ cup light corn syrup
½ cup maple pancake
   syrup
1 cup dark brown sugar
¼ teaspoon salt
¼ cup margarine, melted
1 teaspoon vanilla
3 eggs, slightly beaten
2 tablespoons flour
1 heaping cup pecans

Combine syrups, sugar, salt and vanilla. Stir in beaten eggs and mix well. Stir in flour until well blended. Stir in melted margarine. Pour into an unbaked 9-inch pie shell. Sprinkle pecans over filling. Bake at 350° for about 45 minutes or until set. If top of pie browns before it is done place a piece of foil over the top.

TEXAS PINTO BEAN PIE

1 cup cooked pinto beans
4 eggs
2 cups sugar
1 cup margarine
1 tablespoon vanilla

Mash beans. Beat eggs and sugar together; add margarine, flavoring and mashed beans. Mix well. Pour into a 9-inch unbaked pie shell. Bake at 350° until firm.

PINEAPPLE COCONUT PIE

1½ cups sugar
3 tablespoons flour
3 eggs, beaten
2 tablespoons lemon juice
1 cup coconut
1 cup drained crushed
   pineapple
¾ stick margarine, melted
1 teaspoon vanilla

Mix together sugar and flour. Add eggs, lemon juice and vanilla. Mix well. Stir in coconut and pineapple. Add melted margarine. Pour into unbaked pie shell. Bake at 350° for 1 hour or until set.

GRANDMA'S PRUNE PIE

2 cups cooked
  unsweetened prunes
¾ cup brown sugar
¼ cup flour
¼ teaspoon salt
Grated rind of 1 lemon
Juice of ½ lemon
1 cup of liquid from
  prunes

Cover one pound of dried prunes with 2 cups warm water and simmer until they are tender, adding water if necessary to have one cup liquid when the prunes are cooked. Pit the prunes and cut in half. Combine with the brown sugar, salt, flour and prune liquid. Add lemon juice, rind and sugar mixture to the prunes. Cook, stirring constantly, until the mixture is thickened. Pour into a baked pie crust. Cover with meringue and brown.

OLD-FASHIONED PUMPKIN PIE

2 cups cooked pumpkin
2 tablespoons melted butter
1 cup sugar
½ cup dark corn syrup
½ teaspoon salt
½ teaspoon cinnamon
¼ teaspoon cloves
½ teaspoon nutmeg
½ teaspoon ginger
½ teaspoon allspice
1½ cups milk
2 eggs
1 unbaked 10 - 12 inch pie
shell or 2 unbaked 8-9 inch
pie shells

Mix pumpkin, butter, sugar, syrup, salt, spices and milk. Beat eggs well and add to mixture. Pour into unbaked pie shell. Bake at 425° for 10 minutes. Lower oven to 350° and continue to bake for 50 minutes more.

GRANDMA'S RAISIN PIE

Cook 2 cups of raisins in 2 cups water. Cook until tender. Add 1 cup sugar and 2 tablespoons flour that have been mixed together. Add a pinch of cinnamon and a pinch of salt. Add about 2 tablespoons of lemon juice. Stir all together well.

Pour into pie shell; cover with a top crust. Bake at 400° for 30 to 35 minutes.

FRESH STRAWBERRY GLAZED PIE

1 quart strawberries
1 cup water or 7-Up
1 cup sugar
3 tablespoons cornstarch
Whipping Cream or Cool
  Whip

Simmer 1 cup strawberries and ⅔ cup water or 7-Up for 3 minutes. Blend in sugar, cornstarch and ⅓ cup water or 7-Up. Boil 1 minute, stirring constantly. Cool well. Put 2½ cups of strawberries in a baked 9-inch pie crust. Cover with glaze, making sure edges are sealed. Top with Whiped Cream or Cool Whip.

TEXAS SUGAR PIE

4 eggs
1 cup sugar
1 cup brown sugar, packed
2 tablespoons flour
½ teaspoon salt
½ cup butter, melted
½ cup milk
1 tablespoon vanilla

Beat eggs, sugars, flour and salt together. Add melted butter, milk and vanilla. Pour into unbaked pie shell. Bake at 350° for 50 to 55 minutes or until set.

SWEET POTATO CUSTARD PIE

3 eggs, separated
¾ cup sugar
1 cup hot cooked, mashed
   sweet potatoes
¼ cup margarine
1½ cups milk
1 teaspoon vanilla
½ teaspoon cinnamon
½ teaspoon nutmeg

Beat egg yolks until thick. Gradually add sugar; mix well. Add remaining ingredients; mix well. Beat egg whites until stiff peaks form; fold into sweet potato mixture. Pour into a pie shell. Bake at 350° for 50 minutes or until set.

GILMER SWEET POTATO PIE
(Gilmer is the sweet potato capital of Texas)

½ cup finely chopped
   pecans
2 tablespoons margarine
¼ cup brown sugar
1 cup mashed sweet
   potatoes
¾ cup dark corn syrup
4 tablespoons margarine
½ cup brown sugar
2 teaspoons cornstarch
½ teaspoon salt
3 eggs, beaten
Pecan halves to cover top
   of pie

Combine first 3 ingredients and spread on the bottom of a 9-inch unbaked pie shell. Bake at 450° for 10 minutes; remove from oven and cool.

In a medium saucepan combine mashed sweet potatoes, corn syrup, margarine, brown sugar, cornstarch and salt. Bring to a boil and cook for 3 minutes, stirring constantly. Slowly add beaten eggs and mix well. Pour into pie shell and cover top with pecan halves. Bake at 400° for 10 minutes. Reduce heat to 350° and bake 30 to 35 minutes more or until set.

GREEN TOMATO PIE

3 cups green tomatoes
(about 5 medium)
¼ cup water
1⅓ cups sugar
3 tablespoons flour
4 teaspoons grated lemon
rind
½ teaspoon nutmeg
¼ teaspoon salt
6 tablespoons lemon juice
3 tablespoons margarine

Slice peeled and cored tomatoes in ¼ inch thick slices. Combine tomatoes and water in a saucepan. Bring to a boil then reduce heat. Simmer covered for 5 minutes. Remove tomato slices with a slotted spoon. Mix sugar, flour, lemon rind, nutmeg and salt into liquid in saucepan where tomatoes were. Cook and stir just till boiling. Remove from heat; add butter. Gently stir in tomato slices. Cool 10 minutes. Spoon into unbaked pie shell. Top and seal with pastry and cut slits in it. Sprinkle with sugar. Bake at 400° for 40 minutes.

from Grandma's
Ice Box

FRUIT PIZZA
This is a beautiful dessert and delicious.

Crust:
½ cup butter
3 ounces cream cheese
1 cup flour
⅛ teaspoon salt
2 tablespoons sugar

Filling:
3 ounce cream cheese
¼ cup sugar
1 tablespoon milk
1 tablespoon grated orange
   rind
⅔ cup whipping cream

Glaze:
½ cup sugar
2 tablespoons cornstach
¼ cup water
½ cup orange juice, fresh
¼ cup lemon juice, fresh

Crust:
Soften cream cheese and butter to room temperature. Blend together; add flour, sugar and salt. Blend together well and form into a ball. Press into an ungreased pizza pan with fingertips, press up around edges. Brown at 350° until lightly browned. Cool.

Filling:
Beat first 4 filling ingredients with electric mixer at medium speed until smooth. Gradually add whipping cream, beating until thick and creamy. Spread mixture over cooled pizza crust. Refrigerate while preparing glaze.

Glaze:
Combine glaze ingredients in a saucepan. Cook over medium heat stirring constantly until mixture comes to a boil and is thick and clear. Cook 1 minute. Remove from heat. Let cool while preparing fruit. Arrange a variety of fruits on top of the pizza. I use fresh strawberries, green and red grapes, mandarin oranges and kiwi fruit. Spoon glaze over top of fruit making sure to have all the fruit covered. Refrigerate until ready to serve. It is best if served the same day it is made.

AUNT LOUISE'S STRAWBERRY MERINGUES

3 egg whites, room
  temperature
¼ teaspoon cream of tartar
1 teaspoon vanilla
1 cup sugar
Vanilla ice cream
Strawberries, sliced

Combine egg whites, cream of tartar and vanilla, beat until frothy. Gradually add sugar, 1 tablespoon at a time, beating until stiff peaks form. DO NOT UNDER BEAT! Spoon meringue into 6 equal portions on a well greased baking sheet. Using back of spoon shape meringues into 4 inches in diameter in the shape of a shell with the sides 1½ inches high. Bake at 275° for 55 minutes or until lightly browned. Turn oven off for 1 hour leaving meringues in oven to cool. When ready to serve put a scoop of vanilla ice cream in the center of each meringue and spoon strawberries over the top.

COKE AND CHERRY GELATIN

8½ ounce can crushed
  pineapple
8 ounce jar maraschino
  cherries, cut up
6 ounce package cherry
  Jello
2 cups Coca Cola
3 ounce package cream
  cheese, cubed
1 cup chopped pecans

Drain fruits, save 1 cup of juice; then put this juice in a saucepan and bring to a boil. Mix in Jello until dissolved. Cool. Add Coca-Cola and stir in well. Add remaining ingredients, mix well and chill until firm.

This makes a good dessert served with sugar cookies.

CRANBERRY ORANGE GELATIN

3 ounce package orange or
  lemon Jello
1 cup boiling water
1 cup orange juice
16 ounce jar Cranberry
  Orange Relish
1 unpeeled apple chopped
1 small can mandarin
  oranges
½ cup chopped pecans

Dissolve Jello in boiling water. Add orange juice and refrigerate until almost jelled. Combine remaining ingredients then fold into almost jelled mixture. Pour into 1 quart mold or dish. Chill until firm.

GRANDMA'S BOILED CUSTARD

4 cups milk
6 egg yolks
½ cup sugar
Pinch of salt
1 teaspoon vanilla

Scald milk. Beat egg yolks until light, add sugar and salt. Pour milk over mixture, a little at a time. Strain into the top of a double boiler. Cook over simmering water only until mixture coats a spoon, about 5 minutes., remove from heat and cool. Stir in vanilla.

CARAMEL CUSTARD

2 cups sugar, divided
½ cup boiling water
3 eggs
2 cups milk, scalded
1 teaspoon vanilla
½ teaspoon almond extract

Sprinkle 1 cup sugar evenly in a heavy skillet. Cook over very low heat, stirring occasionally with a wooden spoon. Cook just until sugar melts into a golden syrup. (If cooked too long or too hot the syrup will taste burned.) Remove from heat; gradually add boiling water, stirring constantly. Spoon into 6 custard cups. Beat eggs until frothy. Add remaining 1 cup sugar, beating until well blended. Gradually add milk, beating well; stir in flavorings. Pour custard over syrup in cups. Set cups into a 9x13-inch pan; pour 1 inch of hot water into pan. Bake at 350° for 1 hour or until knife inserted in center comes out clean. Do not overbake, soft center will get firm. Chill 6 to 8 hours. Loosen edges with knife then invert each onto a serving dish.

SIMPLE AND EASY EGG CUSTARD

3 eggs
4 tablespoons sugar
2 cups milk
⅛ teaspoon salt
½ teaspoon almond extract
½ teaspoon vanilla
Nutmeg

Beat eggs well, add sugar and salt, beat again. Add milk and flavoring, stirring well. Pour into baking dish and sprinkle with nutmeg. Bake at 350° for about 40 to 45 minutes.

BANANA PUDDING

½ cup sugar
⅓ cup flour
¼ teaspoon salt
2 cups milk, scalded
2 eggs, separated
1 teaspoon vanilla
About 25 vanilla wafers
4 bananas, sliced

Mix together sugar, flour and salt in the top of a double boiler. Add milk; cook until thick, stirring constantly. Cover and cook for 15 minutes. Beat egg yolks and stir into custard, cook 2 minutes longer. Remove from heat. Add vanilla and 1 banana, sliced, to custard and stir in. Line a flat dish with vanilla wafers, cover wafers with banana slices then pour custard on top. Top with vanilla wafer crumbs or a meringue with remaining egg whites.

AUNT DOT'S BANANA PECAN CRUNCH PUDDING

1 cup sugar
1 cup pecans, chopped
1 egg, beaten
1 package instant vanilla
   pudding mix
1 cup sour cream
1 cup milk
2 bananas, sliced

Combine sugar, pecans and beaten egg. Spread on greased baking sheet. Bake at 350° for 18 to 20 minutes or until golden brown. Cool. Crush and sprinkle half in a 9-inch square cake pan or custard cups. Combine pudding mix, sour cream and milk; beat at low speed of mixer for 2 minutes. Fold in bananas. Spoon over pecan mixture. Top with remaining pecan mixture crumbs. Chill several hours before serving.

OLD-FASHIONED BREAD PUDDING

4 cups milk, scalded
4 cups coarse dry bread
   crumbs
¼ cups margarine or
   butter, melted
4 eggs, slightly beaten
½ cup seedless raisins
½ cup sugar
¼ teaspoon salt
½ teaspoon nutmeg
½ teaspoon cinnamon
1 teaspoon vanilla
½ teaspoon almond extract
½ teaspoon butter
   flavoring

In a large mixing bowl pour milk over bread crumbs. In a small mixing bowl combine all remaining ingredients and add to bread and milk mixture. Mix thoroughly and pour into a greased 8x12-inch pan. Bake 40 minutes or until knife inserted in center of pudding comes out clean. Cut into squares and serve hot with vanilla sauce spooned on top.

I use cinnamon raisin bread for an even richer flavor.

Vanilla Sauce:
1 cup milk
1½ teaspoons cornstarch
   dissolved in a small
   amount of the milk
¼ cup sugar
1 egg, beaten
½ teaspoon vanilla

Vanilla Sauce:
Bring milk to a boil. Add sugar, cornstarch and egg. Cook 1 minutes, stirring constantly. Add vanilla. Cool slightly. Spoon over pudding.

GRANDMOTHER'S LEMON CHIFFON PUDDING

5 tablespoons flour
1 cup sugar
3 tablespoons butter or
   margarine
3 eggs, separated
1 cup milk
¼ cup lemon juice
½ teaspoon lemon rind

Mix flour and sugar. Cream with butter. Beat egg yolks until thick. Add yolks and milk to sugar mixture. Add lemon juice and rind. Beat egg whites until stiff but not dry. Fold into first mixture. Pour into buttered baking dish. Place baking dish in a pan with 1 inch of hot water. Bake at 350° for 1 hour and 5 minutes or minutes or until firm.

TOP OF STOVE RICE PUDDING

½ cup uncooked rice
2 cups milk
2 cups water
Pinch of salt
1 cup sugar
3 eggs, lightly beaten
½ teaspoon vanilla
½ cup raisins
Cinnamon

In a large saucepan combine rice, milk, water and salt and simmer covered. Meanwhile in a medium mixing bowl combine the remaining ingredients. When the rice is soft and has absorbed all the liquids, after about 35 minutes, pour egg mixture into the rice and combine thoroughly. Cook uncovered over low heat 5 minutes. Pour into a casserole or serving dish and sprinkle top with cinnamon.

RICE PUDDING

1¼ cups cold cooked rice
2 eggs
2 cups milk
1 cup raisins
½ cup sugar
¼ teaspoon salt
1 teaspoon vanilla
Dash of cinnamon

Beat eggs until light and thick. Stir in milk. Lightly mix in other ingredients. Place in a buttered 1½ quart casserole. Place casserole in a shallow pan of water. Bake at 350° for 1 hour.

AUNT DOT'S PRALINE SAUCE
(Good served over ice cream)

3 tablespoons butter
1 cup brown sugar, packed
½ cup half and half
1 cup pecans, chopped
1 teaspoon vanilla

Melt butter in a heavy saucepan over low heat; add sugar. Cook 5 to 8 minutes, stirring constantly. Remove from heat and gradually stir in half and half. Cook one minute and remove from heat. Stir in pecans and vanilla. Makes 1½ cups.

NOTES

Index

Index

PUDDINGS & MISCELLANEOUS DESSERTS

Straw Hat Productions
P.O. Box 807
Livingston, Texas 77351

Please send_____ copies of **TEXAS SWEETS FROM GRANDMA'S KITCHEN** at $9.95 plus $1.50 postage and handling per copy. Texas residents add $80 sales tax.

Make checks payable to **Straw Hat Productions.**
Enclosed is my ____ check or ____ money order for $_____.

Name_____

Address_____

City_____State_____Zip Code_____

Straw Hat Productions
P.O. Box 807
Livingston, Texas 77351

Please send ____ copies of **TEXAS SWEETS FROM GRANDMA'S KITCHEN** at $9.95 plus $1.50 postage and handling per copy. Texas residents add $80 sales tax.

Make checks payable to **Straw Hat Productions.**
Enclosed is my ____ check or ____ money order for $_____.

Name_____

Address_____

City_____State_____Zip Code_____

Straw Hat Productions
P.O. Box 807
Livingston, Texas 77351

Please send ____ copies of **TEXAS SWEETS FROM GRANDMA'S KITCHEN** at $9.95 plus $1.50 postage and handling per copy. Texas residents add $80 sales tax.

Make checks payable to **Straw Hat Productions.**
Enclosed is my ____ check or ____ money order for $_____

Name_____

Address_____

City_____State_____Zip Code_____

Reorder Additional Copies